Canoe Tripping and Life:
One Stroke at a Time

By
ALAN M. CVANCARA

Illustrations by the Author

Copyright © 2008 by Alan M. Cvancara

All rights reserved. No part of this book shall be reproduced or transmitted in any form or by any means, electronic, mechanical, magnetic, photographic including photocopying, recording or by any information storage and retrieval system, without prior written permission of the publisher. No patent liability is assumed with respect to the use of the information contained herein. Although every precaution has been taken in the preparation of this book, the publisher and author assume no responsibility for errors or omissions. Neither is any liability assumed for damages resulting from the use of the information contained herein.

ISBN 0-7414-4811-4

FRONT COVER PHOTOGRAPH: On the Pembina River, North Dakota. By Fred Wosick © 1976.

Published by:

//
PUBLISHING.COM

1094 New DeHaven Street, Suite 100
West Conshohocken, PA 19428-2713
Info@buybooksontheweb.com
www.buybooksontheweb.com
Toll-free (877) BUY BOOK
Local Phone (610) 941-9999
Fax (610) 941-9959

Printed in the United States of America

Printed on Recycled Paper

Published June 2008

To Ella:

To whom I rely on for writing ideas, useful word choices, and constructive copyediting–without whose contributions my writing would suffer.

She has delivered me at numerous canoe put-in points and picked me up at numerous take-out points–understandably with reluctance at times, and with concern over my and her safety.

Also by Alan M. Cvancara

A Field Manual for the Amateur Geologist (1985; revised edition, 1995)

At the Water's Edge (1989)

Sleuthing Fossils (1990)

Exploring Nature in Winter (1992)

Edible Wild Plants and Herbs (2001)

Back Trip (2002, with Ella Cvancara)

Windows Into Legacy (2003, with Ella Cvancara)

Bare Bones Geology (2003)

Wildflower Personalities (2004)

Prairie Crocus (2005, novel)

Designs of Nature (2005)

Prairie Crocus in a Man's World (2006, novel)

Geological Glimpses (2006)

Down the Academic High Road (2006)

Down the Road With Dacotah (2008, novel)

CONTENTS

Chapter 1: Some Givens	1
Chapter 2: My C/K Background	7
Chapter 3: My C/K Travel Beginnings and Beyond	18
Chapter 4: C/K Equipment and Travel Techniques	24
Chapter 5: Toward a Total Experience	41
Chapter 6: Experiencing an Entire River by Canoe	53
Chapter 7: Why Solo Travel?	62
Chapter 8: Longer Trips	70
Chapter 9: Thrill of Discovery on the Water	81
Chapter 10: Protected Oceanic Sea Kayaking	89
Chapter 11: C/K Trips That Preview as Reckless	106
Chapter 12: Sense of Trip Urgency	115
Chapter 13: Post-Back-Trauma Tripping	120
Chapter 14: Synopsis: C/K Strokes and Life's Strokes	130
Appendix 1: Canoe and Sea Kayak Travel Log	133

Chapter 1
Some Givens

When I embarked on writing books, I had hoped that my first would be about canoeing. But my potential publisher, Prentice-Hall, showed little interest in such a book, much less any book of mine. But after a long delay, the publisher allowed me a stab at a popular geology book, which has proven the most successful of all of my writing efforts. Now, many books later, a renewed desire has sparked alive and tugged me into writing the neglected canoe book. Some of life's given strokes, like paddle strokes, may seem wasteful or valueless at the time, but evolve as enlightening ones.

Actually, this book deals with more than basic canoeing. I emphasize tandem canoe travel, to be sure, but also delve into solo canoe and sea kayak tripping as other means of self-propelled water travel.

I focus canoe/sea kayak (C/K) travel mainly on learning about nature. Running rapids may thrill me as this adrenaline rush thrills other canoeists, but I don't travel the watercourses just for the excitement. I go mainly for the bald eagle's snowy head-tail-flash, the loon's cry, and the orca's blow.

And sometimes I'm treated to nature's aesthetic impressions. On one late-in-the day kayak swing along Cass Lake, Minnesota's well-vegetated shore, a near-setting sun burned an orange-red beam on barely rippled water. Silhouetted bulrushes punctuated exclamation points against the blazing sky. My closed eyelids couldn't block shimmering reflections as I sensed the last sun-warmth on my face. At sundown, four loons crossed my path on the water within 30 feet of me as an anemic moon gained ruddy complexion to cast a yellow-pinkish-rippled beam on the water.

Loons at moonrise.

Besides learning *about* nature, you can learn *from* nature. On a late July day, I learned how to maneuver my sea kayak within 25 feet of a great blue heron on the Crow Wing River, Minnesota, near First Crow Wing Lake. With binoculars to my eyes, I inched in closely enough to make out the bird's black pupils and yellow irises. This largest of North American herons spent most of its time waiting with mouth agape, and stared intently for prey with its head hunched on shoulders. I learned to wait, and make my advances only at times when Big Blue moved: to pick at plant debris, shake its wings, or jab its long beak for a fish. As the heron stalked its prey, I stalked the heron. I ignored the time spent on this lesson, thankful for the opportunity. A master teacher of patience, the heron taught me the real meaning of the word. Eventually the bird got its fill or I crowded its bio-space, and my avian professor winged off.

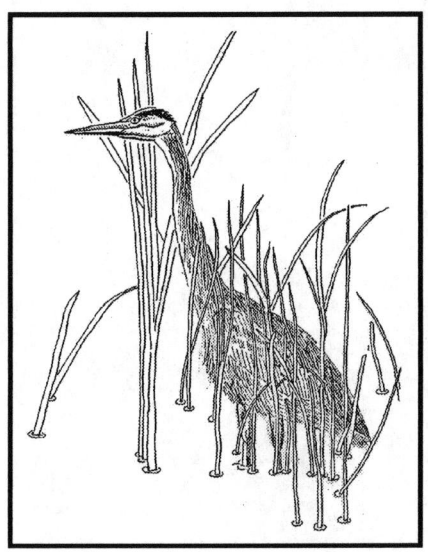

Patient great blue heron in waiting.

On my C/K travels, especially on solo trips, I've always tried to live at the moment, notably conscious of outside awarenesses. John O. Stevens, in his book *Awareness: exploring, experimenting, experiencing*, recognized three kinds of awareness: awareness of the inside (AI), awareness of the outside (AO), and awareness of fantasy (AF). Awareness of the inside while on a C/K trip includes any awareness on the inside of the body–sore shoulders from paddling, full bladder, pained back from a lengthy portage, or a hunger pang. AO deals with any awareness on the outside of the body: sunburn, a bulging-eyed leopard frog resting at a quiet, duckweed-covered stream surface, the hoo-WHAAH-hoo of a loon's wail. And AF refers to any thought or idea–in the past, present, or future–that may occur while paddling.

A great blue heron stalks a leopard frog in duckweed.

What might we learn from the relative proportion of awarenesses that comes to us? If most of your awarenesses fall into the AO category, you've satisfied your body's needs, you're in relative comfort to enjoy yourself, and you're living at the moment–a desirable place to be. Relative comfort relates to wearing the appropriate clothing for your selected trip, choosing a route that's not overly ambitious for your physique, and pacing your paddling so as not to burn out before the end of the trip. If, on the other hand, a large proportion of awarenesses fall within the AF group, you might be overly fantasizing about the past or future, and allowing living at the present to slip away.

I've been on C/K trips during which compatriots have dwelt on events that have happened, that will happen, that may never happen–all while paying little attention to the magnificent scenery and fascinating life. I attempted to soak up the natural experience in spite of the human-created ambience, and recorded the highlights.

Some C/K journeys, billed as "float trips," may be little more than that. The stream acts simply as a conveyor belt to sweep humans from point A to point B. Shallow water and bottom become disturbed, and so do the often-littered banks. If you're just downstream from such a watery gala, the shouting and paddle-slapping of the water precedes the flotilla long before it screams into view. In like manner, the "sport" of "tubing," riding of floating inner tubes, elicits similar noisy behavior. Oftentimes liquor flows as freely as the stream's current.

In such situations, wildlife scatters for cover. Witnessing nature at those times becomes hopeless. You select another time, another day for your travel.

Although I think of C/K tripping primarily as a means to further enlighten me about nature and its workings, such travel offers parallels with life's journey, as reflected in the title of this book. These aquatic journeys can serve to help educate you about yourself and how you might deal with adversity.

Paddle strokes, discussed in Chapter 4, can relate directly to strokes in life. At the end of each chapter, I'll philosophize a bit, and attempt to relate C/K tripping to life tripping. You'll find this section headed *Application to Life*.

Chapter 2
My C/K Background

As a reader or potential reader of this book, you may ask me: What are your qualifications to write this book? A fair question. I'll lay it on the line, and let you judge for yourself.

The canoe and sea kayak travel log in Appendix 1 summarizes my experience in self-propelled water travel: more than 1,900 miles on 78 trips in seven states and one Canadian province during 1965-2000. I don't look upon this as some kind of record, and I didn't set out for a record. I simply enjoyed water travel and secured as much as time allowed. Where I mention trip numbers, they refer to those listed in Appendix 1.

Maps accompanying this chapter show the watercourses that I traveled. Water miles top the list in northern Minnesota at 754 and central and eastern Montana at 622. I generated most of my water miles while residing at Grand Forks, North Dakota. But the water courses in that state didn't appeal as much to me, either because of their being less attractive or less permanent.

From the beginning, something compelled me to record details of my C/K travels. So, I can now corroborate what took place on these trips. Taking notes requires extra effort after a hard day's paddle, but you're glad you did when you desire to relive a trip. Chapter 5 delves into record-keeping.

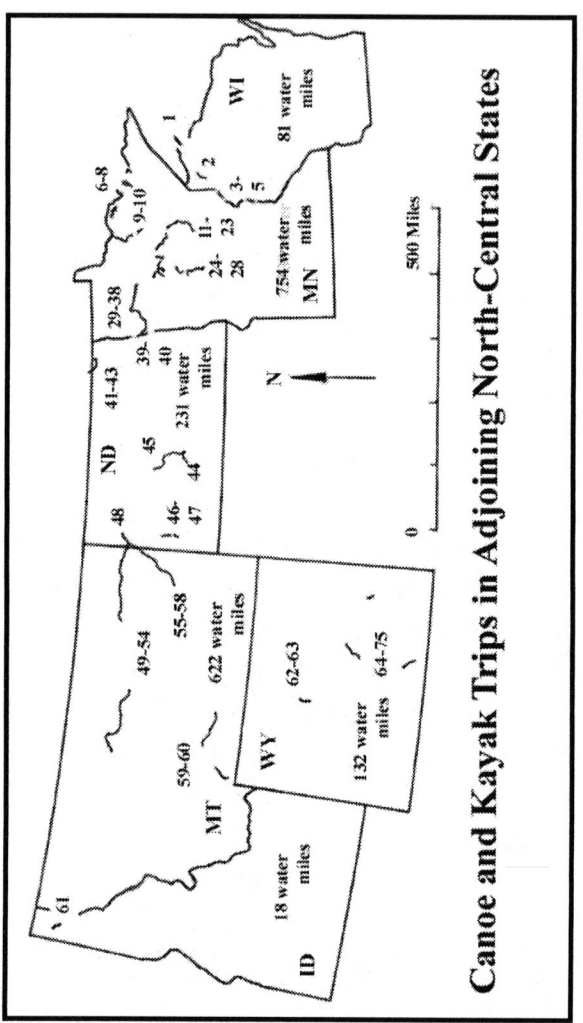

My numbered C/K trips, stream segments, and water miles in six adjoining north-central states. Appendix 1 give details.

In spite of my C/K background documented in Appendix 1, this compilation doesn't tell the whole story. Repeats of several trips or parts of trips do not appear in the total tally.

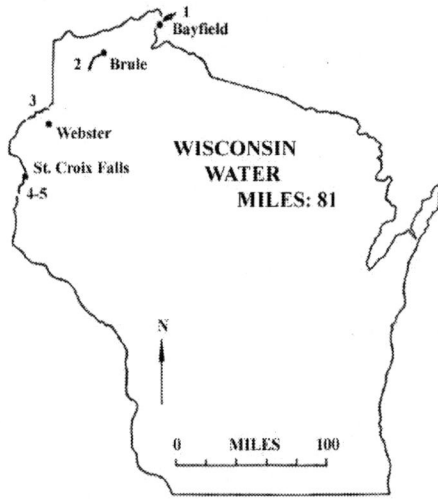

Location of my C/K trips in northwestern Wisconsin. Trips 3 to 5 are also shown on the following map of Minnesota. Appendix 1 gives details.

And notably what doesn't appear in Appendix 1 constitutes the numerous hours on the water to gain firsthand experience for writing my freshwater ecology book, *At the Water's Edge*. During parts of the springs and summers of 1984-1986, I devoted more than 100 hours in a tandem canoe, solo canoe, and sea kayak on Minnesota streams and lakes for background research for the book. I say "more than 100 hours" because I can document at least 100 hours. In addition, though, I logged many additional hours but, somehow, my note-taking broke down. And I can't substantiate them either by the amount of time on the water or by the distance traveled. Some of the trips recorded by time on the water stand out as intensive to me now—up to 7 hours in a day.

The variety of experiences on the water as background for the book can be gained from a series of less-often acquired vignettes.

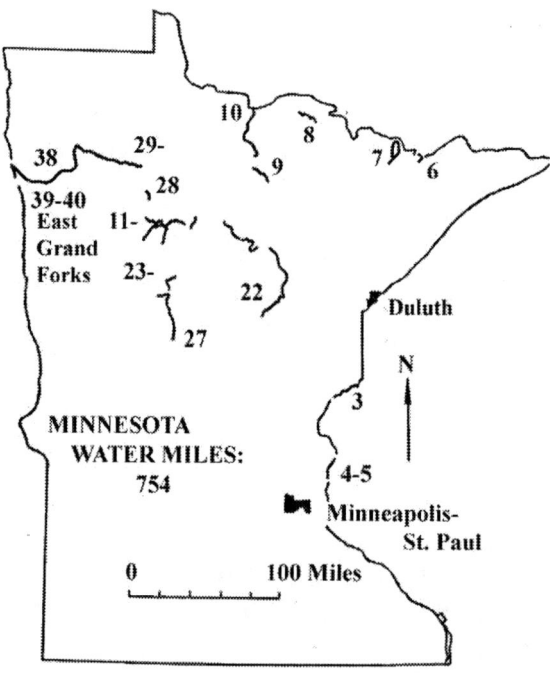

Location of my C/K trips in northern Minnesota. Trips 3 to 5 are also shown on the preceding map of Wisconsin and trips 39 and 40 on the following map of North Dakota. Appendix 1 gives details.

Vignette 1: One cool morning on the Necktie River northeast of Laporte, I came upon a dew-spangled spider web attached to sedge leaves and dipping into quiet water. The land-derived sedge and spider web were succumbing to consumption by the aquatic ecosystem. Energy flow takes place through re-cycling of matter as some organisms die so that others may live.

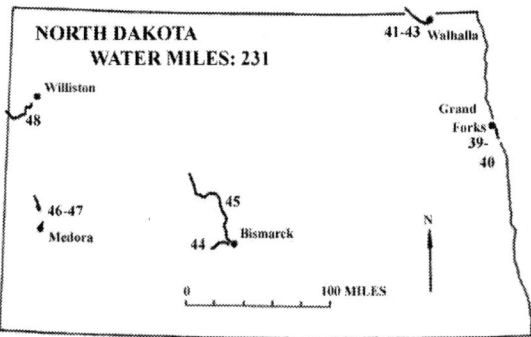

Location of my C/K trips in North Dakota. Trips 39 and 40 are also shown on the preceding map of Minnesota. Appendix 1 gives details.

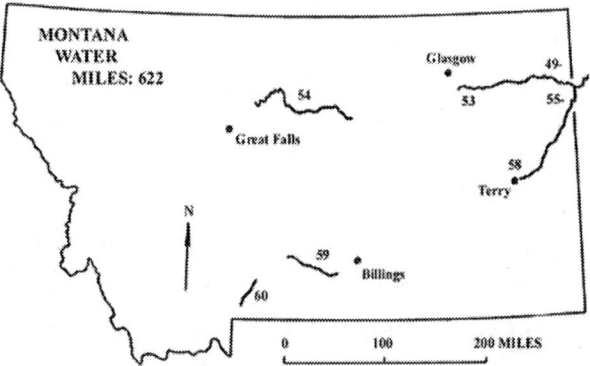

Location map of my C/K trips in central and eastern Montana. Appendix 1 gives details.

Vignette 2: Not likely recognized by most persons, I witnessed several freshwater sponges from my watercraft. Freshwater sponges appear mostly as encrusting masses on rocks or plants, and feel rough to the touch, not like slimy algae. Colors vary from white

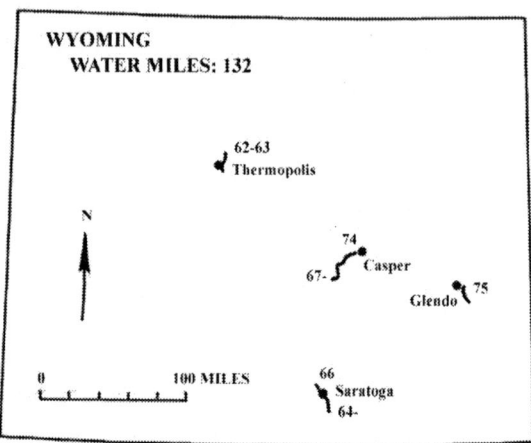

Location of my C/K trips in central and southeastern Wyoming. Appendix 1 gives details.

to cream to brown, showing green only when algae live with them. They're made up largely of sharp, microscopic needles of silica called "spicules." Don't rub your eyes after handling them! On Little Boy Lake and Little Boy River, I found sponges attached to bulrush stems and small alder–strangely growing in the water. On the Pelican River, bright green and creamy white sponges encrusted boulders and cobbles.

Vignette 3: At the edge of Elbow Lake, a mink sat on one of several remnants of pilings 10 inches above the water. It would dive from its piling perch repeatedly but always returned to its claimed piece of real estate. At one point the mink, like a bullying human, snarled at a painted turtle on a neighboring piling and frightened the reptile away. All of the mink's antics took place as if I weren't there.

Dipping dew-spangled spider web partnered with a frog.

Vignette 4: I often relished the presence of swimming muskrats and beaver from my canoe or kayak, each animal creating an obvious wake. A too-close approach to a beaver would elicit a slap on the water by its paddle-like tail and submergence. On the Crow Wing River near First Crow Wing Lake, a swimming beaver crossed my bow within 25 feet. At the south edge of Two Island Lake, a large beaver lodge served as a favored spot to witness beaver activity. I might see two or more beaver in the water at the same time or observe them climb onto the lodge.

Vignette 5: On a cooler than normal morning in July–I could see my breath at the put-in–I cherished a magical time on a stream draining Oak and Little Horseshoe Lakes. Fog at first blocked out the stream ahead of me, nearly choked by wild rice. Mink frog calls came out of the fog, slower initially, then speeded up as the temperature rose. A bittern squawked overhead.

Vignette 6: At Little Horseshoe Lake, just offshore, a loon sat on her nest planted in floating sedges. Before I attempted a photograph, the bird fled with much chatter and commotion to expose a single egg. I fled, too, ashamed at scaring her from the vigil with her egg.

Vignette 7: On another cool morning–in my kayak by 6:30 a.m.– fresh, moist air at Hart Lake and Necktie River seemed to cleanse me as if I were breathing water. Super dewdrops rode floating wild rice leaves. Under certain light they resembled highly mobile drops of quicksilver. Upturned edges of the leaves temporarily contained the dewdrops, but they quickly slipped away with the slightest movement. I wondered: Could the large dewdrops have "grown" by the accretion of smaller drops on the waxy leaves? A loon foursome escorted me as I pondered the question, but proved too skittish to photograph. Flecks of pinkish-red and yellow wild rice blossoms adhered to my kayak as I headed away.

Vignette 8: I saw painted turtles regularly but snapping turtles only on occasion. One warm day in May at Blackbird Lake, I witnessed a snapper swimming underwater. When aroused by my passing kayak, it left a foot-wide "trail" of tiny bubbles on the water's surface.

Vignette 9: I'm always thrilled to find creatures on the defensive or feeding. Near the outlet of Carmen Lake, a bald eagle perched in a live white pine 75 yards from its nest in a dead white pine higher than half way up. When an osprey approached the nest tree, the bald eagle chased it away. Moments later, with less serious intent, the osprey attempted to drive off the eagle. Still in the vicinity of Carmen Lake, I spied two porcupines ambling along a sedge mat at the edge of Lower Egg Lake. One stopped and began munching on a white water lily leaf.

Devoting numerous hours in watercraft for background research for *At the Water's Edge*, I also used the opportunity to acquire photographs for the book. A canoe or kayak serves as a good photographic platform. With only a breeze from a favorable direction, I've been able to drift within useful photo-shooting range of a swimming loon in open water. The paddle should be stowed and body movements kept to a minimum. But don't approach such a quarry too closely. Signs of nervousness–constant chatter, repeated rapid movements, and suggestion of flight–indicate that you are trespassing within the bird's discomfort range. The bird may resort to a "penguin dance" escape maneuver, illustrated in Chapter 5.

For nearshore subjects from a motionless watercraft, a short length of light rope with a clamp attached proves useful. Clamp onto bulrushes, cattails, or other larger, rooted aquatic plants, and snug the free end of the rope up to the plant to maintain the watercraft in place.

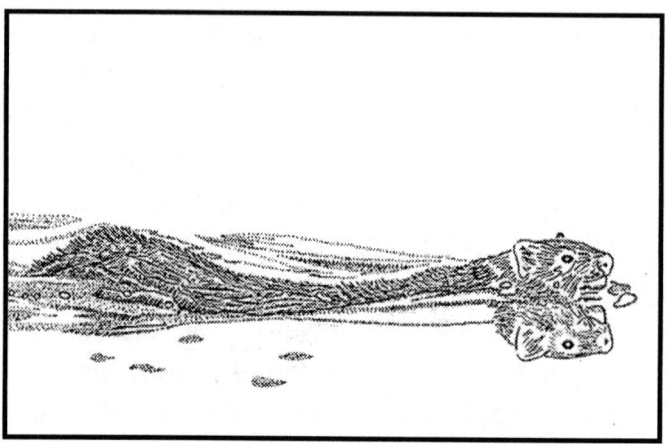

A swimming mink, slicing through morning calm water, caught originally on film from a sea kayak.

    A memorable photographic experience with my sea kayak as the shooting platform sticks in my mind. The scene: the marshy upper part of the small Larimore Reservoir in northeastern North Dakota. During a morning cruise in my kayak, I followed a narrow strip of open water. Guttural sounds to my left fractured the relative quiet of the place. Something told me to grab my camera with telephoto lens from my pack. I let the momentum of the kayak carry me forward and waited. In moments, a mink thrashed through the marsh vegetation to the right. Astonished by its appearance, I almost forgot about the camera. But I squeezed off one shot as the animal swam directly in front of me within the narrow window of open water. No time for a second shot–impossible also because of that being the last exposure on the roll of film. My field notes say: "May have gotten a photo of a mink." The photograph shows a mink in its wake with head reflected in the water. And good enough to introduce Chapter 11 of *At the Water's Edge*.

Application to Life: Whether work or passion, you develop qualifications to carry out either seriously. Sometimes your passion becomes your life's work. A case in point: Verlen Kruger, record-setting, marathon canoeist. Although initially a plumber, his passion for canoeing led him to the Cross Continent Canoe Safari (1971) across Canada and Alaska; the Ultimate Canoe Challenge (1980-1983) across much of the U.S. and Canada including traveling the Grand Canyon *upstream*; the Two Continent Canoe Expedition (1986-1989) along the length of both North and South America; and various records during the Mississippi Challenges (1984, 2001, and 2003). He paddled 100,000 miles. And his passion eventually led to his designing and making canoes.

Chapter 3
My C/K Travel Beginnings and Beyond

Because of having been raised a lone child on a North Dakota farm, my wife says that I've had an incomplete childhood. Some toys and experiences just didn't come my way. This smacks true for canoes and canoeing. I didn't enter the world of canoeing until 1959 while a member of an air crew in a jet fighter via the U.S. Air Force. The place: Glasgow Air Force Base, northeastern Montana.

But my first canoe proved more of a joke as a watercraft. Labeled "The Minnow," I remember it as about 13 feet long. Actually, I assembled it from a kit. The fiberglass hull came as a single piece, but I had to fashion the wooden decks, thwarts (cross supports), and gunwales (GUN-nelz; upper edges of the canoe's sides). The shallow hull didn't allow for seats, so you sat on the bottom of the canoe. I selected this short, light-weight model especially for solo travel.

Because The Minnow seemed inherently tippy and I lacked canoe experience, I avoided the nearby Missouri River below Fort Peck Dam. After eventually canoeing below the dam in another craft, I'm glad I stayed off the Missouri early on. Instead, I puttered around in the sluggish Milk River, and went on no real trips. Ella paddled in The Minnow, but felt unsafe in it. On one occasion, my father-in-law accompanied me in this now-realized-as questionable watercraft. To this day, I can't imagine why he did.

I acquired my first real canoe in 1965, a 15-foot, tandem or two-person aluminum craft that weighed 54 pounds. Again, as for The Minnow, I selected this canoe especially for eventual solo travel. This canoe saw a plethora of water miles, as evidenced by numerous scratches from rocks. I still have this craft. I've been criticized for owning such a short, slow watercraft. But I would take this reliable canoe on almost any reasonable freshwater body.

I embarked on my first canoe trip, a combination of trips 23 and 25 on the Shell (15 miles) and Crow Wing (18 miles) Rivers in central Minnesota. My wife, Ella, accompanied me on this 3-day affair in September, 1965. I had hoped we would travel on many joint trips. The first day proved fine, but the second dawned with overcast skies and remained that way all day–with intermittent light rain. We supported the overturned canoe on two picnic tables, and sat under it all day. At times, the campfire smoke drifted under the overturned canoe, and elicited coughs from us. We concentrated on food, and tried several options, such as baking bread on a stick over hot coals. Ella remained quiet most of the day, but opened up the next as the weather improved. I enjoyed the clear water, with visible moving sand and freshwater mussels on the bottom. Painted turtles, muskrats, ducks, and great blue herons appeared often.

In August, 1966, Ella and I continued another 34 miles (trip 27) on the Crow Wing, downstream from Anderson's Crossing where we stopped in 1965. This time, weather proved fair for our 3 days, and we enjoyed the river and its life as we had on the first and last days of the 1965 trip.

In August, 1972, with another couple, we overlapped part of the 1965 and 1966 trips on the Crow Wing, and extended our travel downstream (trip 26). Between Anderson's Crossing and Nimrod, faster current corresponded with frequent submerged boulders that scratched the bottom of my canoe. Aluminum "smears" on many boulders testified to other canoeists experiencing the same problem.

At our camp below Nimrod, wintergreen grew abundantly under pines. We made a fine tea by steeping rounded tablespoons of torn leaves–one per cup–in hot water for 5 minutes.

Clouds increased, light rain began about midnight.

Following a hurried breakfast, we broke camp in light rain. Ella and young son, Mark, apparently in their haste in the rain, fell in the river while boarding the canoe. The dumping soured wet dispositions even further. We hurriedly paddled the remaining 5 miles to Oylen in rain.

As for the 1966 Crow Wing trip, we had our Siamese cat Si'm with us. But the rain blemished his experience as it did ours. He huddled beneath the stern seat from where I paddled. But my being heavier, rainwater collected beneath my seat, and Si'm crouched and shivered in the cold water.

When we reached the take-out, the bridge at Oylen, I grabbed Si'm and tossed him out of the canoe. We all busied ourselves unloading gear and packing it into our vehicle. We ignored Si'm. When ready to leave, Ella asked, "Where's Si'm?" We spread out, searched the brush and heavier woods, called his name repeatedly. No answer. Ella and I exchanged pained looks.

Mark said, "We can't leave without him."

But we had no choice. We returned the following weekend, inquired of local residents about him. Some said they had seen a strange Siamese cat, but knew nothing of his present whereabouts. We never saw him again, and he left a serious void in our lives.

We explained Si'm's departure as his opportunity to seek freedom. When we let him outside, he never roamed independently—always on a leash. Maybe he and we all paid for this error.

Ella canoed with me one other time during my working years, an 11-mile day trip (trip 34) on the Red Lake River in May, 1966 with another couple, Don and Alice. Being pregnant, Alice often felt the urge to urinate. Each time, she sought the need to relieve herself in some vessel. So we all searched for a can at several stops. Eventually she and the rest of us tired of these searches, and she did the deed without an unnecessary, intermediary container.

Ella's reluctance toward further canoe tripping hinged around her comments: "It always rains on canoe trips. It's often too hot. I can't keep clean." I suspect canoeing in rain on two trips, topped off with losing our cat Si'm on one rainy trip, clinched her stand against further time on the water. She would rather devote time to life's challenging strokes rather than to paddle strokes.

In fairness, I must mention Ella's continued link with my C/K tripping. She delivered me to numerous put-in points, and picked me up at many take-out points. This, at times, when her other activities were affected, and at remote sections of streams where she detested what might await her.

With Ella unavailable as a water co-traveler, I requested friends, relatives, and my two children as paddling companions. And, as a geology professor, I coerced my students on other trips—at times an entire class! In those cases, canoeing served as a means to complete a justifiable field trip.

I can't explain my dallying with latching onto a kayak—a 17-foot sea kayak to be specific. This didn't happen until 1984. Once obtained, though, I spent hour after hour in it, especially to gather background for my book *At the Water's Edge.* This craft proved ideal when going solo. With low bow and stern, it caught less crosswind than my canoe. And the double-bladed paddle made travel in wind easier as well. Protection against rain worked particularly well. A spray skirt sealed me in the cockpit, and a raincoat over the spray skirt provided a completely dry ride. As for the aluminum canoe, I still have the sea kayak.

Liking a craft propelled by a double-bladed paddle, I followed the sea kayak 2 years later with a 16-foot solo canoe. Not that I *needed* two canoes. You sat in the middle of the solo canoe, and could make slight fore-aft corrections in positioning the seat. But this craft was totally open like my tandem canoe, so I opted for the sea kayak most often when heading out on solo trips. Ella couldn't understand the sensibility of my three-craft armada, I'm sure. She could easily have avoided paddle strokes altogether after her two wet excursions.

Application to Life: I might raise the analogy of dating with the beginnings of C/K tripping. You take out a date to dinner, possibly a movie, discover likes and dislikes, feel out each other's dispositions. If all goes well, you might date a few more times, test each other a bit further. By this time, the relationship should either click or falter. With canoeing or kayaking, you undergo a similar period of testing. If you can't leave it alone, you're hooked.

Chapter 4
C/K Equipment and Travel Techniques

Canoeing

If you're new to canoeing or kayaking, this chapter will aid you in selecting equipment and provide travel techniques.

Canoes come in several designs. You select that design which corresponds to your principal use. If you're reading this book, you likely might prefer a tandem, day-tripper or weekender canoe of medium volume to easily carry two people and their gear. A good length would be 16 to 17 feet. If you desire a faster craft, select a narrower one over 17 feet. For extended trips, a high-volume wilderness-tripper canoe exceeding 18 feet might be the answer. If you expect rough water use, choose a canoe that's 12 inches deep or deeper for a drier ride. And avoid those craft with high ends that catch wind and add weight.

What about stability? Flat-bottomed canoes may seem stable at first, but may tip readily if you lean markedly to either side. On the other hand, they maneuver well. Round-bottom craft feel tippy at first, but tend to resist capsizing, especially if heavily loaded. They also paddle easier. For best stability, avoid canoes with strong side bulge and inward curve toward the upper edges–called "tumblehome" by the experts.

Keels resist abrasion, provide rigidity, and improve tracking. But they tend to hang up a canoe on rocks in swift water and make quick turns more difficult. If a keel comes with your choice of canoe, select one with a shallow-draft shoe type.

Keel line shape or the fore and aft rise of the canoe's ends–also called "rocker"–may be a design factor to consider. A canoe with least rocker tracks the best but doesn't turn well, and responds slowly to rising incoming waves.

If solo canoeing ranks primary on your agenda, choose a craft 16 feet long or less that weighs about 50 pounds or less. You'll likely have to compromise speed for less weight.

Give some consideration to hull material. A few craftsmen still fabricate expensive wooden and bark canoes. But the wooden canoes tend to be heavy. Lighter, abrasion-resistant aluminum canoes demand little or no maintenance. But they're noisy–screech through bulrushes, clunk from carelessly placed paddles–and cold to the touch.

Most canoes today derive from various synthetic materials. Polyethylene plastic hulls resist impact and abrasion well, but detract by being heavy. Composite hulls of fibers impregnated with plastic resins surpass others because of their strength, light weight, and capability to be molded into various forms. Fibers can be of fiberglass, carbon, or other non-glass material. These composite hulls, however, remain relatively expensive.

You go nowhere without a paddle, so its selection becomes as crucial as the canoe. You're apt to devote countless hours with this tool, an extension of your arms. As for length, some say equal to the "nose-to-toes" dimension when standing. I prefer a length closer to toes-to-collarbone or toes-to-armpit. But length depends on personal preference and in what part of the canoe you intend to spend more time. A stern paddler requires a slightly longer paddle because of sitting somewhat higher.

Select a paddle blade with a smoothly-rounded central thickening that tapers gradually toward the edges. This design allows for greater control and efficiency as the blade passes through the water–like a streamlined aircraft wing passing through air. Blade widths vary from about 6 to 10 inches, with the wider blades better for touring.

Other paddle considerations: Oval shafts feel better than those circular in cross-profile. And evaluate the grip. Which is better for you, a rounded-palm or T-grip?

Wooden paddles, of a single piece of wood or laminated strips, have become largely replaced by those of synthetic materials. Wooden paddles tend toward greater weight and narrower blades, and those of laminated strips tend to separate. The lighter, stronger paddles have shafts of aluminum or synthetic fiber and blades of such fiber.

Now for the launching. If with a partner, lift the canoe off the vehicle, and, while maintaining the upside-down position, position each end on a shoulder. Place the corresponding arm along the side of the canoe and grasp it at the keel line. Don't allow the canoe to rock from side to side. This only makes the carry more difficult. On a long haul, the stern person may slip totally under the craft and rest a gunwale on each shoulder while the bow person guides the carry. A low cut bank offers the ideal launching site. Allow the canoe to roll off your shoulder and that of your partner sideways toward the water, and let it slide down a thigh. Tie in a spare paddle, and place the to-be-used paddles at the far side of the craft.

Final launching depends on the water body. In flowing water, direct the bow downstream. If your partner is the bow person, he or she should step in on the keel line in a crouch to keep the center of gravity low, and grasp the gunwales. You steady the canoe against the cut bank. With your partner settled, you step in similarly, and, with a push, shove off. On a low, sloping beach, you and your partner pick up the canoe near the middle on opposite sides, and direct it, bow first, into the water by hand-over-hand passing. Your partner and you embark in a way similar to that on streams. I'm not fond of launching from beaches—especially rocky ones—because of scraping the canoe's bottom, possibly slopping water into the craft, and often wet feet or shoes.

If alone, grasp the canoe at midsection, and gradually slide it off your vehicle toward you. Depending on the height of your vehicle, you may have to stand on a sturdy stool. Position the center thwart behind your neck and partly on your shoulders. Pad your shoulders with a heavy shirt, jacket, life vest, or permanently mounted shoulder pads as used for portaging. Tip the bow slightly upward to see your way forward. At the water's edge, grasp the inside of the gunwale or the center thwart on the side toward the water, and the center thwart on the opposite side. Roll the canoe over as you shift your head and shoulders away from it. Slide the craft down on a thigh. Bend your knees so as not to strain your back.

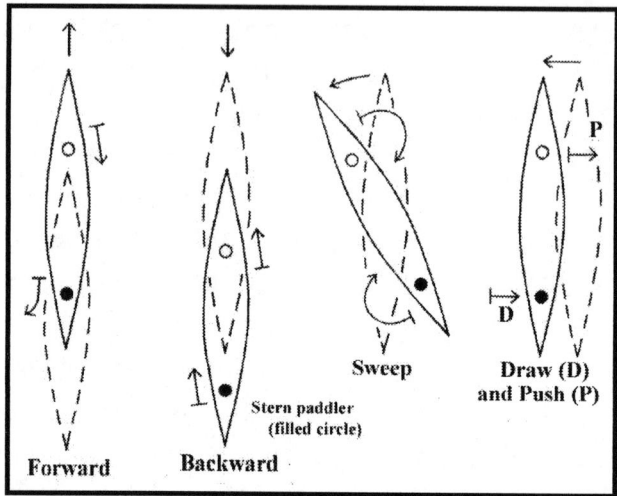

Basic paddle strokes. Open circles designate the bow paddler, filled circles the stern paddler. Cross lines on arrowed lines that indicate paddle movement show orientation of the blade. On the far left, the stern paddler modifies the forward stroke to a J-stroke to maintain the canoe's course.

Five paddle strokes serve to propel and guide your canoe in lakes and slower streams. With the forward stroke, which carries the canoe forward, you draw the paddle parallel to the keel line and toward the rear of the canoe. Enter at a high angle to get a good bite on the water, and immerse the blade at least three-fourths of its length. The stern paddler does most of the steering. His or her forward stroke generally transforms to some variation of the J-stroke: The paddle traces the letter J parallel to and outward from the canoe as it passes the canoeist's hips. This aids in steering at the completion of the forward stroke as the paddle also acts as a rudder. Slight pressure on the blade in either direction maintains the canoe's course, especially if the stern paddler matches the timing and force of the bow paddler.

Tandem canoeists generally paddle on opposite sides, and change sides at will. When changing sides, careful canoeists avoid dripping water into the canoe. The bow paddler does this by swinging the paddle in front of the bow, the stern paddler by rotating the paddle behind his or her back. An experienced solo canoeist maintains a straight course with a forward J-stroke on one side of the craft, and changes sides only infrequently.

The backward stroke allows you to move rearward without turning the canoe around. For fast reversal, precede it with a braking action. Hold the paddle vertically in the water, against a gunwale for more efficient stopping.

A sweep stroke allows you to turn in a wide circle in quiet water, easiest done in the stern. The blade traces a wide arc from a gunwale and back again. To turn the canoe effectively to the left, for example, the stern paddler makes a reverse sweep on the left while the bow paddler accompanies with a forward sweep on the right.

Draw and push strokes provide the means for turns and lateral shifting of the canoe in running water. In a draw stroke, you reach out to the side, set the blade at a high angle, and draw the paddle in toward yourself. The canoe shifts toward the paddle. Simultaneous left stern and right bow draws *rotate* the canoe to the right. Simultaneous left stern and left bow draws *shift* the canoe to the left. Such would be a maneuver if a damaging rock loomed quickly on the right side. The cross draw provides a rapid optional maneuver. If a bow person paddling on the right spots a threatening rock on the right, he or she quickly crosses his or her paddle over the bow and draws in on the left. The stern paddler complements the cross-draw maneuver by drawing in on the left.

With a push stroke, you place the paddle vertically in the water and push it away from you. The canoe responds by moving in the opposite direction. You and your partner may combine draw and push strokes. A simultaneous left stern draw and a right bow push shift the canoe to the left. A pry stroke offers a trickier alternative to a push stroke. You hold the blade vertically in the water, as for a push stroke, but against a gunwale. Pry against the gunwale to lever the canoe sideways. Probably best to avoid at times, this stroke may cause a capsize in rough, rocky water.

In fast water, well coordinated duo paddlers course their canoe past rocks and partially submerged tree trunks through deeper water as if guided by a huge, transparent hand. An alert bow paddler initiates corrective action via draw, cross draw, or push strokes. Sensitive to the bow paddler's movements, the stern paddler quickly responds with well-chosen complementary strokes. Nonverbal communication may soar to unparalleled levels. So, from all of this paddling discussion, a few strokes allow you to travel a plethora of water bodies.

Knowing how to read rough, running water helps negotiate it. To read it, you must understand its language. You usually hear difficult water before you see it: a sound above that of the wind that may increase to a dull roar which forebodes nasty rocks, a dam, or a waterfall. Some admonish: Never stand in a

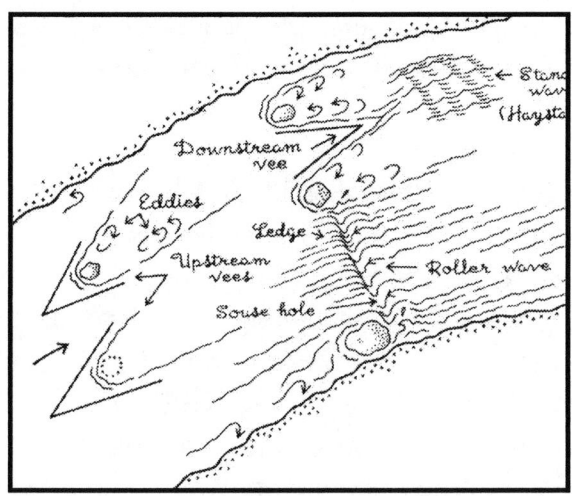

Reading swift water for negotiating safe passage. The safest passage passes between the two upstream vees and through the downstream vee. The closer upstream vee portrays a submerged rock.

canoe! But I've done it numerous times from the stern. Just spread your legs to the sides of your canoe, slowly rise from your seat, and bend your legs slightly for best balance. This tactic allows me to size up rough water a bit sooner than if I remained in my seat.

Start your evaluation by following the rule of vees. A vee that points upstream reveals a rock, projecting above the water's surface or submerged a few inches. Two nearby rocks form a downstream-pointing, darker vee that usually signals deeper water and safe passage. Expect "standing waves" or "haystacks"– waves that remain stationary–at the apex of a downstream-pointing vee where faster, shallower water meets slower, deeper water. You can usually run low haystacks but direct your canoe along the edges of high ones. If caught in extremely fast water, advanced canoeists seek out the protection of eddies below obstructions where turbulent water opposes the main flow. This allows them time to search for the next downstream vee.

Direct your full attention to a clear waterline across a stream ahead of you. This indicates a sharp drop caused by a rock ledge, dam, or waterfall. Scratch off running a waterfall immediately, and don't be tempted by the ledge or dam. Both may be followed just downstream by a "souse (SOWSE) hole," a trough scooped out by fast water, and a "roller" or "keeper wave." Aptly named, the keeper wave "keeps" you in its grip as it rolls in reverse *toward* the drop-off at the surface and away from it at the bottom in a continuing cycle.

If rough, running water clearly seems uncanoeable, you have a couple choices to skirt it: lining or portaging (PORE-tihge-ing). But first, scout your detour route well for high cut banks, partially downed trees, or large rocks.

Lining involves guiding a canoe along shore with ropes or lines fastened to the bow and stern. Each line, or painter, should be about 25 feet long, kept neatly coiled, and fastened to the bow and stern, to be used also for tie-up at stops. A quarter-inch rope of braided nylon works well. You can line your canoe with or without removing gear. One painter per canoeist works best, but one canoeist may handle both painters, which is necessary for solo travel. Don't allow the canoe to align broadside to the current in fast water or you may lose control of it, but manipulate the painters so the current works for you in guiding your craft around obstacles.

Portaging or carrying your canoe and gear is generally a safer method to avoid rough water unless you meet a bear, sprain an ankle, or encounter some other mishap. If your canoe lacks cushioned pads or a portage yoke at the center thwart, lash two paddles to the center and bow thwarts. With the blades at the center thwart, the paddles form a vee with the open end facing the bow. The blade-shaft junction of each paddle should rest on each shoulder.

Unless your canoe is unduly heavy, a single canoeist can usually portage it more readily than two—especially over irregular terrain. For easiest mounting of the canoe, have your partner raise the upside-down craft high at the bow as the stern rests on the ground. You slip under the canoe at the center thwart, grasp it forward at the gunwales and carry it away. If alone, reverse the solo launch mentioned earlier. Grasp the canoe amidship, one hand on the inside of the gunwale closest to you, the other at the far end of the center thwart with the palm facing in the direction of the portage. Place your feet well apart for good balance, one forward of the other, and bend your knees to favor your back. With the raised canoe resting on a thigh, place your near hand on the center thwart. Flip up and twist the canoe over, and position your shoulders under the center thwart.

Sometimes you portage not to avoid treacherous water but simply to complete parts of a trip. On my second trip (trip 7) to the Boundary Waters Canoe Area of northeastern Minnesota, my partner, Andy, and I had to negotiate 10, 6, and 7 portages on days 1, 3, and 4 of a 4-day trip. He, 20 years younger, carried the canoe while I double-packed our Duluth packs. Mosquitoes and rain plagued us on some of our portages.

We thought our longest portage, 300 rods or 0.94 of a mile, a bit of a challenge. But this pales in light of portages made by Verlen Kruger, mentioned before, and Steve Landick, while on The Ultimate Canoe Challenge. At one portage, they each carried their separate craft and gear *30 miles* in North Dakota from the Garrison Dam on the Missouri River to the Souris River near Velva. At another, they portaged *66 miles* in Wyoming from the South Pass area to the Popo Agie River. On the North Dakota portage, Verlen carried canoe, pack, and gear all at the same time. But on the Wyoming portage, he had to use the leap-frog approach: Carry his canoe for 15 or 20 minutes, then return for his pack and gear. So, he, in fact, covered the same ground *three* times!

Let's imagine a run through fast water which you've opted instead of lining or portaging. You've secured your life vest on and stowed the painters so you don't become entangled in them. As the rapids loom closely, you and your partner might kneel to lower the center of gravity. Keep the paddle in the water as much as possible for greatest control and stability. You might return the blade from a forward stroke while in the water, and feathered parallel to the keel line. If the canoe tends toward tipping on your paddling side, apply a low "brace." Lean over and brace your paddle at a low angle with the blade flat against the surface of the water. The low brace acts like a stabilizing outrigger. If the canoe tips away from your paddling side, apply a high brace. You lean out over the water, and thrust the blade vertically as for a draw. But you anchor the blade out there, facing the side nearest you against the current for best stability.

Always be aware of alternative tactics. If the current swings you completely around, don't panic. Be ready to ride the rapids backwards. This may seem a bit frightening, but can be done; it's happened to me at least a few times. If you hang up on a rock, shift your weight fore and aft, and you may be able to slide or push off. At times, you might be able to step out on a rock, free your craft, and step back in quickly without capsizing.

And, if you capsize? First, *stay upstream* of your canoe. A water-laden craft can pin you against a rock from which there may be no escape. Try to maintain a grip on your paddle. Float downstream on your back with your legs extended downstream so they contact obstacles before other, more vulnerable parts of your body do. Hang onto your canoe if it remains free, and attempt to maneuver it to shore.

You can propel your canoe with other than a paddle. Poling involves use of a 10- to 12-foot pole with a steel shoe at the business end. Earlier wooden poles have been replaced, in part, by lightweight aluminum poles.

Poling provides another excuse for standing in a canoe. First, try this out in shallow dead water with the pole in hand. You might also try walking the length of the craft until you feel confident about your balance. Try poling in water largely choked by vegetation where a paddle would likely become entangled.

Some advanced canoeists pole their crafts in shallow, rocky streams where a paddle would easily become damaged. And they readily travel both with and *against* the current. For this kind of travel, they follow the rule of thumb of always keeping more weight at the downstream end of the canoe to help maintain control in a current. Going downstream, current takes a firmer grip on the heavier bow. Going upstream, current grasps the heavier stern more firmly. Before you attempt poling in swift, rocky water, you might extract a few tips from an experienced poler.

Reading standing water involves only basic perception. But wind- and large boat-generated waves require taking some precautions and tactics. To avoid strong winds, stay near shore and on the leeward sides of islands and peninsulas. Travel earlier in the morning and later in the day when winds tend to offer less hindrance.

If caught in strong head wind waves, or those generated by large boats or ships, angle the bow at about 45 degrees to them. This better allows the bow to ride over the waves rather than slice directly through them. Power your forward strokes to slightly lift the bow with each oncoming wave. Watch constantly for the wind's tendency to broach the canoe and whip it broadside. A tail wind often provides a welcomed luxury, but a strong one can swamp you. Prevent this by angling the stern as for a head wind, and trim the stern so it rides higher. You can also prevent rear broaching by attaching a sea anchor, such as a pail or cooking pot, to the rear painter. I prefer a collapsible canvas pail.

Kayaking

To many self-propelled water travelers, kayaking offers an easier alternative than canoeing, and greater intimacy with the water. Generally lighter and faster than canoes, kayaks can be readily moved through the water and steered with a double-bladed paddle. On trip 8 in the lakes of Voyageurs National Park, Minnesota, my son and his friend, both in their late teens, paddled a 15-foot aluminum canoe. I traveled solo in a 17-foot sea kayak. They could never keep up with me, much less surpass me. This comparison points out how design differences affect propulsion in the two craft.

Kayaks, as well as canoes, come in several types. Shorter, shallow, quickly maneuverable kayaks fit white-water thrill-seekers, who expect to get wet in these craft. Longer, deeper kayaks designed for touring serve better the aquatic naturalist. Cockpits sit higher than the ends for rain and splash to drain away from them. Nylon or rubber spray covers that fit snugly around a cockpit and you–coupled with a rain jacket and hood– provide a dry ride. For The Ultimate Canoe Challenge, Verlen Kruger designed a craft that resembled a kayak as much as a canoe, but fitted with a long, roomy cockpit completely sealed with a spray cover. Waterproof hatches, fore and aft, should be considered for stowing food and gear in compartments. Construction materials for kayaks parallel those for canoes.

Select a double-bladed kayak paddle with as much care as you would a canoe paddle. Various recommendations relate to paddle length. I say begin with a paddle length that equals the distance from the bottoms of your feet to the fingertips of an upward-extended arm. Adjust this length after you've tried several paddles. Consider both the more rigid single-shaft paddles versus the less rigid take-apart paddles. As for kayak hulls, paddles come in several materials.

Kayakers debate about feathered versus unfeathered paddles. Some profess the greater efficiency of feathered paddles–with blades at right angles to each other. Others point out that feathered paddles produce greater wrist and arm strain, and aid the paddler only in head winds. You might begin with a single-shaft, unfeathered paddle, and carry a spare, compact take-apart paddle to experiment with feathering.

Launching a kayak differs a little from launching a canoe. Two people remove the upright-transported kayak at the bow and stern from racks on a vehicle similarly as for a canoe. If alone, roll the kayak partly over, grasp it on either side of the cockpit, and lift it off the racks. Carry the craft by resting an edge of the cockpit on a shoulder, and steady it with a hand on the same side. Lower the kayak to a thigh, and slip it, bow or stern, into the water.

You'll find entry into a kayak trickier than for a canoe. As for canoes, select a low bank for an ideal launching site. Using your paddle as a brace, place part of the shaft across the craft at the rear edge of the cockpit and another part with a blade lying flat on the bank. For entry from the left, grasp together the rear lip of the cockpit and the paddle shaft with your right hand. With your left, press down on another part of the shaft against the top of the bank. Maintaining balance, slip your right leg into the cockpit, followed by the left. Shift your body and slide into the seat.

With your initial entry into the water, you might sense a kayak as tippier than a canoe. So strive for good balance, and keep your hips and backbone flexible.

Apply essentially the same paddle strokes in kayaking as for canoeing. Try to match the strength of your forward strokes on each side to avoid frequent course corrections. To make a slight course change, hold a blade toward the stern as a rudder. If a high wave swings you broadside, lean *into* it and apply a brace.

Because you're more apt to capsize in a kayak, practice an escape maneuver, preferably in a warm pool or lake. For added insight into the experience, wear a skin-diving mask and snorkel. Snug the spray cover around your life vest. Hold your paddle along the side of the kayak. Lean into a tip-over. When you hang upside-down, allow yourself to slip down and away from the cockpit. The spray cover will come away with you as you leave the kayak. Keep a grip on the paddle as you float to the surface. If some distance from shore, upright the kayak, stow your paddle, and attempt to reoccupy your seat. Come directly behind the cockpit, and, with a thrust, shove your body up and across the kayak. Twist to the right or left, slip one leg into the cockpit, followed by the other. Shift your body into the seat. All the while, try to maintain good balance.

Many kayakers stress learning the Eskimo roll as a safety, self-righting tactic following capsizing. You recover from a tip-over while on the move. For some, this requires considerable practice, and may be difficult to execute during an emergency and in cold water. By all means acquire the roll if you're so inclined, best learned from an instructor or veteran roller.

Application to life: Paddle strokes can be likened to life's parallel strokes in developing a career. Forward strokes make positive steps toward your goal, backward strokes set you temporarily in reverse. Draw and push strokes allow you some lateral shifting in your choices, J-strokes keep you on course, sweep strokes allow you some major turns along the way, and braces provide defense against major upsets. Power or easy paddle strokes equate to much or little effort in seizing your life's goal.

Each stroke, paddle or life, may seem like only a minute increment. But persistent strokes can lead to colossal accomplishments, depending on the effort expended. In the early 1980s, Verlen Kruger and son-in-law partner, Steve Landick, pulled off what they called The Ultimate Canoe Challenge in North America: 28,000 miles! Verlen paddled 50 to 60 strokes per minute in his power-stroke mode—which meant only 4 mph. But his continued persistence paid off.

And don't resist furthering canoeing's or life's strokes because of age. Kruger had reached 58 when he began the ultimate canoe trip. And I know of a black mandolinist who left his assisted living facility in his 90s—and bought a new banjo to extend his music background..

The finely-tuned skill of highly coordinated tandem canoeists in challenging swift water can be likened to life's activities developed by two or more in-step persons: rancher husband and wife on a cattle drive, father and son playing musical instruments, teacher and student recording bird behavior. Highly sensitive to each other's behavior, they all perform their work instinctively with little obvious communication.

Chapter 5
Toward a Total Experience

Travel by canoe or kayak can be fulfilling in simply going from one point to another, especially if combined with other activities such as fishing or photography. But we may be further rewarded by opening up to all that's around us. We may never attain a total experience on a water trip, but we can work toward it. The key to striving toward such an experience hinges around knowing how to observe, and building on a backlog of lifelong events and adventures.

As you travel, devote all your senses to your environment: the black-, white-, and red-flash of a rose-breasted grosbeak; the rattle of a squirrel or woodpecker; the odor of creosote as you approach a wooden bridge; the cool breath of a breeze on your cheek; the sweetness of serviceberries lingering in your mouth. Allow these senses to operate freely as you dip your paddle and continually keep an eye on the water. Scan your surroundings for a time, focus on a part, then scan again. Be open to every awareness that comes to you, and allow it to register for you to record later. Follow a mental checklist with which to group the awarenesses, as described in Chapter 1. While paddling, jot down any details that you think you may forget, such as a running list of birds.

Wildlife identification stems foremost, but also animal behavior which reveals deeper insight. Watch for wildlife especially in the early morning and late afternoon or evening. And since riparian wildlife tends to sense less fear from the water traveler than the land traveler, you're more apt to approach it closer from your watercraft.

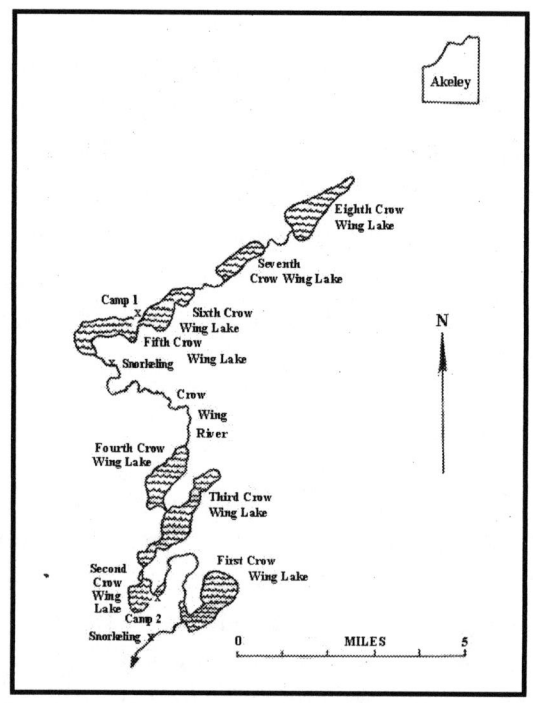

Crow Wing Chain of Lakes and the Crow Wing River in northwest-central Minnesota.

To perceive what and how you might glean a wealth of information while on a C/K trip, let's focus on the Crow Wing Chain of Lakes connected by the Crow Wing River in northwest-central Minnesota, nestled south and west of Akeley. The lake chain trends southwest, and the Crow Wing River generally flows in that direction as well. Labeled simply by numbers, the Eleventh Crow Wing Lake rests at the northeast end of the chain adjacent to Akeley, the First Crow Wing Lake at the southwest end. My son, Mark, and I paddled the 24-mile route between the Eighth and First Lakes, he in a solo canoe, I in a sea kayak. We devoted 3 days to the trip in early August. I supplemented what I learned on this cruise by personal visits to seven specific points along the chain in late July and early September of two other years.

Field notes provide a record of what you've experienced, and should be written with some care with an attempt toward completeness. But the relative completeness depends on your mood, the weather, your background with nature, and your attitude toward note-taking.

Most people align into two groups for trip records: the Memory Recorders (MRS) and the Johnny Inkslingers (JIS). Memory Recorders simply rely on their memory. But the Johnny Inkslingers write copious notes. I suppose I'm classed among the JIS. During the days of the legendary lumberjack, Paul Bunyan, Johnny Inkslinger served as a conscientious accountant for a mythical lumber company. From his name, you can surmise that Johnny kept complete and detailed records. Some persons fall somewhere between the MRS and the JIS, rely much on memory, but take a few notes.

The human mind has the remarkable ability to store information and recover it, but also stands out as notorious to forget–particularly details. Upon reviewing my field notes, I'm amazed at the details that I've forgotten. When I re-examine my better field notes, I'm able to relive my nature experiences so much more fully.

If recording by the written word seems too much of a chore, capture your spoken word by means of a cassette tape or digital recorder. But this means of recording entails disadvantages. Cassette tape recorders may involve tangled, broken, or dunked tapes. Both types of recorders may be damaged by water, and need to be monitored for spent batteries. And both types likely involve cataloguing and storing recorded observations.

Because field notes tend to be disorganized, I find it useful to group observations into categories. I prefer a notebook 5 by 7 ½ inches with stiff covers, and a heavy-duty wire binder that allows the pages to lie flat when opened. The pages should be of good quality paper in case the notebook gets wet. I write with a medium-hard pencil. If harder, the pencil grooves; if softer, the lead smudges.

To demonstrate how an account of a trip may change with the amount of information and how it's organized, I'll first give the bare bones field notes of such a trip, then follow this with an organized transcription which includes supplementary notes from other visits. In both cases I write in telegraphese style to cut down on the effort and save space.

Crow Wing Chain of Lakes and Crow Wing River, Southwest of Akeley, MN
[Field Notes]

August 3 to 5, 1986
Crow Wing Lakes and River, southwest of Akeley MN

Trip with Mark. He used solo canoe, I used sea kayak. River high. Weather warm, partly cloudy, westerly (light) winds. Rain in evening and at night of 8/4.

Route includes ~ [about] 24 miles of all or parts of 8 Crow Wing lakes and associated Crow Wing River. Put-in at NE edge 8th CW Lake, take-out on river (where crossed by rd 109) below 1st CW Lake.

8.5 hours paddling time for average rate of 2.8 mph. Not difficult to traverse lakes; crossed 8th Crow Wing and 4th Crow Wing Lakes in 40 and 35 minutes.

Plants: Cattails (leaf tips beginning to turn brown), reed grasses, wild rice (lower part of fruiting spike blossoming; mostly 3-5 ft above water but approaching 7 ft at one place), white water lilies (blossoms abundant), yellow water lilies (near end of blossoming period), arrowheads (blossom), coontails, duckweeds, waterweeds, pondweeds, Joe pye-weeds (blossom), swamp milkweeds (blossom), wild irises (green seed pod state).

Vertebrates: Mallards, blue-winged teals, loons, gulls, cormorants, great blue herons, kingfishers, turkey vultures, hawks, eastern kingbirds, red-winged blackbirds.

Other: Currants, blueberries available (probably late for these).

Crow Wing Chain of Lakes and Crow Wing River, Southwest of Akeley, MN]
[Organized and Supplemented Account]

Note: See field notes for 7/26, 28, 29, 30/84; 9/3/84; 8/10/85; and 8/3-5/86 (canoe/kayak trip with Mark).

Environment: Chain of lakes connected by slow river. Eleven lakes total, but traveled only through eight. Much of route wooded. Put-in at upper end Eighth Crow Wing Lake, take-out below First Crow Wing Lake where Hubbard Co. 109 crosses river. Paddled 24 miles in 8 ½ hours for average rate of 2.8 mph.

Weather: For canoe/kayak trip, warm, partly cloudy, light westerly winds. Rain in evening and at night of 8/4.

Aquatic plants: Four zones on river (from riparian to open water): Riparian DOGWOOD and ALDER zone>SEDGES zone (with cattails, reed grasses, and bulrushes)>WILD RICE zone (with yellow and white water lilies)>OPEN CHANNEL.

Other riparian plants: Beggar ticks, Joe-pye weeds, swamp milkweeds, nettles, wild irises.

Other plants: Docks, arrowheads, water arums, horsetails, greater duckweeds, lesser duckweeds, star duckweeds, water meals, coontails, bladderworts, water milfoils, waterweeds, spikerushes, pondweeds, bur reeds, jewelweeds. Zones in lakes similar to those in river but water lilies and water milfoils more prevalent; also mare's tails, stoneworts, buckbeans, mud plantains.

Invertebrates: Water striders and whirligigs (both on surface film), snails (*Lymnaea stagnalis* or great pond snails, *Bulimnea*, *Physa*, *Helisoma*), freshwater mussels (black sandshells, fatmuckets, plain pocketbooks), pill clams (*Pisidium*), scuds, damselflies, dragonflies (seen mating in flight), stonefly nymph cast "skins" (on stump), crayfish (feeding on dead, whitish northern pike), sponge (white, attached to wood; resembles coral head).

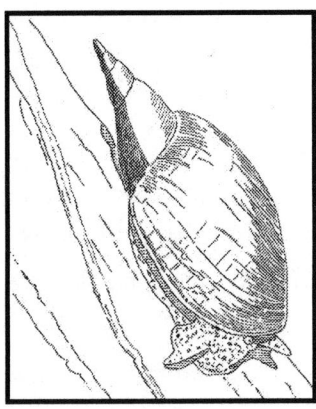

Great pond snail, one of the larger freshwater snails that approaches 2 ½ inches in length.

Birds: Mallards, blue-winged teals, wood ducks, loons (visual and call), gulls, cormorants, great blue herons, kingfishers, turkey vultures, hawks, eastern kingbirds, red-winged blackbirds, swallows, catbirds (call).

Other vertebrates: Walleyes, northern pikes (up to about 2 ft), perch, bluegills, green sunfish, rock basses, largemouth basses, crappies?, redhorses, suckers, carp, minnows, bullheads, johnny darters, painted turtles, beaver, muskrats.

Other: Currants and blueberry fruit. Showed Mark how to clean cooking pot with hard, silica-bearing horsetail stems at Camp 1, at inlet of Fifth Crow Wing Lake. Camp 2 at east edge of Second Crow Wing Lake. On 9/3/84, five canoes with Native American "ricers" put in below First Crow Wing Lake. Of each of three young couples, man sat with paddle or with sticks to rap wild rice into bottom of canoe. Woman stood behind him with long pushing pole fitted with short branches or duck-bill-like contraption to get grip on bottom.

Sensations:
1. Smooth glide of kayak over and through water lily pads.
2. Slap and rub of bulrushes against kayak hull.
3. While snorkeling, marked consciousness of breathing as air rushes through snorkel. Sunlight streaming into water, dying in darkness. With diving mask, seeing both terrestrial and aquatic worlds at same time.

Impressions:
1. Like the variety of paddling from river-to-lake and lake-to-river many times.

The detail to which you note organisms depends, of course, upon your familiarity with various groups. I'm stronger with plants, snails, and clams than birds. Others would outshine me in their listing and knowledge of behavior of birds.

Besides recording an overview of aquatic plants according to zones, as I've done, you may group them as to whether they rise above the water, remain submerged, or float on the surface of the water. Here's a sampling:

Emergents	**Submergents**	**Floating Leaf Plants**
Sedges	Coontails	White Water Lilies
Cattails	Bladderworts	Yellow Water Lilies
Bulrushes	Stoneworts	Duckweeds
Arrowheads	Pondweeds	Watermeals
Bur reeds	Water Milfoils	
Spikerushes	Waterweeds	
Wild Rice		
Horsetails		

To stress ecological relationships, you might record plants and animals as they habituate together. Your categories may be Riparian Life, Surface Film Life, Nearshore Life, and Offshore Life. Riparian Life encompasses that on the banks of streams, ponds, and lakes. Among the riparian animals would be turtles, snakes, frogs, salamanders, raccoons, otters, mink, and moose.

Surface Film Life dwellers associate directly with the water's surface, either above or below that surface. Water striders and whirligig beetles—both insects—often stand out as the most conspicuous creatures that live on the upper surface of the watery film, along with duckweeds. Whirligigs gyrate in circles; they, along with some spiders, scamper and dance at will on the water's surface—dimple the surface film but don't break the surface tension. Look for them in standing water and along the quieter edges of slower streams. They cast six-blobbed, halo-fringed shadows on a shallow bottom.

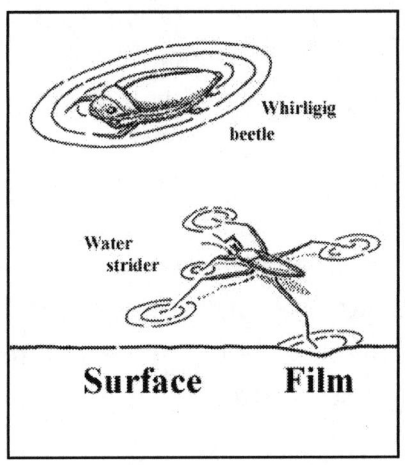

Two dwellers on top of the surface film.

Creatures also inhabit the underside of the surface film. They include mosquito larvae and pupae, and such other insects as backswimmers and diving beetles.

Nearshore Life might include the emergent, submergent, and floating leaf plants along with the associated animals. Among the animals: immature and mature insects, scuds, crayfish, snails, clams, various shorebirds–such as great blue herons and bitterns, fish, muskrats, and beaver.

Offshore Life lies in the open water beyond the Nearshore Life. On the surface we find loons, ducks, gulls, and the like. Below dwell various fish as well as mussels in the shallower depths.

Now, back again to walking on the water's surface, such as by water striders and whirligig beetles mentioned before. The Gospels have attributed to Jesus the miracle of walking on water, for which complete agreement doesn't exist. Loons, though, have the capability to *run* on the water's surface in offshore environments. They resort to this tactic when clearly disturbed, and run in a vertical position called a "penguin dance." I approached loons too closely a couple times to trigger this behavior, and felt ashamed afterward.

I touched on snorkeling previously. This allows for greater intimacy and sense of the freshwater environment. I snorkeled at two pools, one below Fifth Crow Wing Lake, the other below First Crow Wing Lake. Observations about the fish, mussels, and sponge came while snorkeling.

A loon performing a "penguin dance," an escape maneuver.

Unless you're strapped for space in your craft, drop in a diving mask, snorkel, and flippers. In a slow stream with clear water, you can learn much more by snorkeling than just by paddling. I found a good stream for snorkeling to be the Crow Wing River below the Lake Chain in the vicinity of C/K trips 25 to 27. You, of course, would have to avoid rapids, and your partner should scout the stream in advance of your float for safety's sake. In essence, your body becomes its own watercraft, guided and propelled, in part, by flippers. You could record some of your observations, on the float, with a white plastic sheet and grease pencil.

Application to Life: Learning to observe nature with all of your senses provides good training to identify the essence of your fellow humans. How many times do we observe humans closely enough to determine the color of their eyes? And are we cognizant of details in their behavior? How they seem quick to challenge you, how they roll their eyes at one of your remarks, come in close to you at times, back off at others. Pick up their signals quickly and avoid unpleasantness later.

Conversely, look for the positive association gleaned from the true smile, touch of the hand, or discussion of a disagreement without becoming upsetting.

Chapter 6

Experiencing an Entire River by Canoe

The opportunity to truly understand the personality and workings of a river comes from traveling its *entire* course. I've had that opportunity with the Red Lake River in northwestern Minnesota. For me to cover its 193 miles, though, required 10 trips (29 to 38) over a period of 9 years. These trips don't tell the entire story, however, because a few trips overlapped and others I repeated. The longest trip of 78 miles, a 4-day affair from the river's source to St. Hilaire, I paddled alone.

An overview of the river from source to mouth can be encapsulated as: sluggish to faster to sluggish, and with clear water yielding to turbid water. A profile along the river's channel begins essentially flat–because the river originates at Lower Red Lake, steepens noticeably in the vicinity of rapids below St. Hilaire to nearly Crookston, and becomes gentle again towards its mouth. Rivers that begin in mountainous regions have profiles that differ in sharp contrast: steepest at the source, then gradually flatten toward the mouth.

For the first 18 miles, the river courses through the Red Lake Indian Reservation. While portaging around the dam at river mile 181, 12 miles into the reservation, one of two white fishermen asked me: "Did you get permission to canoe on the river?"

"Permission? From whom?" I questioned.

"The Reservation."

"Didn't know I needed permission," I muttered.

"Yeah, well," the other fisherman interjected, "a couple guys were fishing near here in a boat and some Indians took potshots at 'em. Not sure if they had permission, either."

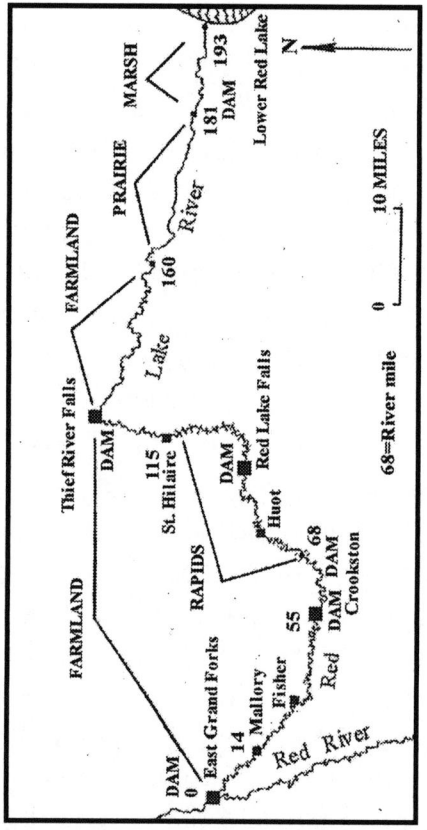

The Red Lake River in northwestern Minnesota.

My mind raced. *Can't go back. Ella's scheduled to pick me up in 4 days. And at St. Hilaire, not at Lower Red Lake. Got no choice, gotta press on. Besides, can I believe what they're telling me?* "Guess I'll take my chances," I reply to the two fishermen.

The remainder of the day, I maintained a low profile, and not just because of the strong wind. I found that I could pass by people living on the bank without their noticing me. That night I camped at the edge of an alfalfa hay field, made *no* campfire so as not to attract attention, and gave thanks for the intermittent light rain throughout the night that might keep persons from wandering about in my direction.

I arose early the next morning, and embarked on the river without breakfast. When my map clearly showed me west of the reservation, I relaxed and ate.

Variable terrain fringes the river. Above the dam and mile 181, where I made my first portage, aquatic plants almost choke the channel, and little suitable terrain for campsites exists. Below the dam, prairie flanks the river with few small trees—mostly willows with balsam poplars, cottonwoods, and boxelders. From near mile 160 to Thief River Falls, generally continuous cottonwood, elm, aspen and willow trees fringe riverbanks and intersperse with fields. Below Thief River Falls, the river courses through farmland.

For the first 2 days of the initial 78 miles, I fought a brisk northwesterly wind. The river flows generally west-northwest between its source and Thief River Falls. Less experienced at the time, I mostly clung to the left bank, and used my paddle as a pole against the bank or paddled from the bow seat. In hindsight, I should have placed considerable weight in the bow or poled the canoe. I paddled 14 miles in 6 hours the first day for an average rate of 2.3 mph.

On the most difficult second day, I received no aid from the current. In places, my canoe would be blown upstream if I ceased to paddle. I managed a rate of only 2.2 mph, 22 miles in 10 hours.

The wind slacked off on the third day, but continued from the northwest. River current remained very slow. But my paddling rate averaged a bit more, 2.8 mph.

The fourth day resembled the third, again with a similar slow current, and I averaged 2.5 mph. The portage around the dam at Thief River Falls proved short but steep. I ended the trip at the north edge of St. Hilaire, at river mile 115.

In the faster 18-mile stretch between St. Hilaire and Red Lake Falls, the river drops 110 feet, reflected, in part, by rapids. In October of the same year, Pete, a graduate student, and I averaged 3.5 mph on this stretch. We found the most exciting rapids in the lower one-third of this river's segment. We misjudged the rapids twice to get hung up on boulders.

The International Scale of River Difficulty places rapids into six classes. The rapids section on the Red Lake River, from about mile 114 to 68, falls in Classes I and II:

> "*Class I.* Easy. Waves small, passages clear; no serious obstacles.
>
> *Class II.* Medium. Rapids of moderate difficulty with passages clear. Requires experience plus suitable outfit and boat."

For comparison, Class V is "exceedingly difficult, long and violent rapids, . . ." Class VI is "unrunnable."

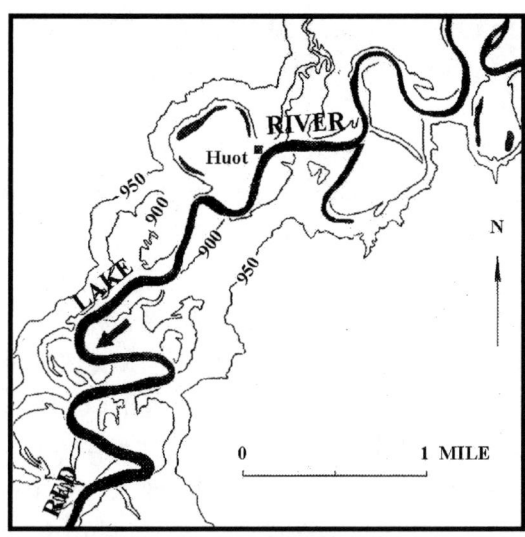

The Red Lake River at Huot, mile 78, displays many river bends or meanders. Meanders cut off from the main channel contain oxbow lakes. The 950- and 900-foot topographic contours delineate the river valley and cut-off meanders.

I've canoed the Red Lake Falls to Huot segment four times, the first time alone when my paddling rate averaged only about 2 mph. Faster water on the third and fourth trips, for comparison, resulted in paddling rates of 6.4 and 4.4 mph with tandem paddlers. Higher water level on the third trip concealed all rocks. Water slopped into the canoe twice from high waves. On the second trip, I paddled in one of six tandem canoes. One struck a partially submerged fallen tree and capsized in cool, mid-September weather. The two paddlers rushed to a nearby farmhouse for warm-up.

Numerous river bends or "meanders" characterize slow streams such as the Red Lake River. They especially prevail from the middle reaches, or say the Red Lake Falls-Huot stretch, on down. Meanders cut off from the main channel may contain "oxbow lakes" or dry up to develop into "meander scars."

My recollection of the river segment between west of Gentilly to Crookston (trip 34) remains strong because of the behavior of a pregnant friend of my wife and mine. Alice and her husband, Don, accompanied Ella and me in their tandem canoe. Her condition necessitated that she urinate frequently. Fair enough. But she felt the need to urinate in a container, which she initially took with her, a large can. Later, she lost the container, and the rest of us felt obligated to search for one at each stop. With eventually only a small can available, Alice finally realized the futility of attempting to urinate into a container. She simply headed for the nearest bush or tree to relieve herself, and ignored the direction of her stream.

Sand-gravel bars and islands mark the river in the middle reaches from below Red Lake Falls to a point between Crookston and Fisher. Shells of mussels concentrate on bars, along with the live animals.

When I see concentrations of mussels, I like to ponder the relative success of mussels versus humans in terms of each group's equipment. Mussels, kinds of clams and rather lowly invertebrates, lack a head, much less a brain and eyes. They've inhabited Earth for more than 200 million years. Humans, depending on when you wish to mark their beginnings, have populated Earth for only a small fraction of that time. The modern species, *Homo sapiens*, has been around for less than a million years or so. The handful of other known species in the family of humans, Hominidae, date back to a mere 5 million years or so. Mussels, too, have diversified in much greater numbers, 300 species in North America alone. Humans, by polluting water bodies, have threatened or endangered the existence of many mussel species. To what extent may mussels have evolved without the intervention of humans?

High cut banks can be found at several places just above St. Hilaire to about Crookston. At such places the river tends to become narrower, deeper, and faster. Sediments in the cut banks consist of clay, silt, sand, and gravel–to boulder-size–laid down by melting glaciers and in a huge glacial lake. Flat farmland, through which most of the river flows, represents the bottom of that glacial lake. Slumping occurs more conspicuously along the high cut banks but remains obvious at low cut banks as well along much of the river. From between Crookston and Fisher to the river's mouth, cut banks remain relatively low, about 20 feet or less.

I mentioned portages around dams at mile 181 and at Thief River Falls. The canoeist must also portage around dams at Red Lake Falls, above and at Crookston, and at East Grand Forks. None of the portages, however, is overly difficult.

The final, sluggish, 13-mile segment of the river from Mallory to East Grand Forks I canoed with John, a colleague. You get a good idea of the degree of meandering by realizing that the river distance comes out as twice the air distance of 6 ½ miles. Sighting two snapping turtles on the banks stood out as the highlight of the trip (38).

Now, for a selected, composite list of some of the plants and animals to be seen along and in the river:

Trees and shrubs: Willows, cottonwoods, boxelders, balsam poplars, aspens, birches, green ashes, basswoods, bur oaks, American elms, roses, snowberries.

Nonwoody riparian plants: Catnips, wood nettles, tall nettles, jacks-in-the-pulpit, columbines, butter-and-eggs, wood sorrels, golden alexanderses, bedstraws, Canada anemones, dame's rockets.

Aquatic plants: Water buttercups, arrowheads, coontails, water milfoils, cattails, reed grasses, white water lilies, yellow water lilies, bur reeds, horsetails, bulrushes, sedges, spikerushes, smartweeds, sweet flags, wild rice.

Edible wild plants: Wild grapes, chokecherries, wild plums, hawthorns, gooseberries, wild asparaguses, Jerusalem artichokes, cattails, arrowheads, wild rice, docks, boxelders (sweet sap for syrup), elm mushrooms, shaggy mane mushrooms. I almost always take note of wild edible plants while C/K tripping–just in case I might return and have to survive on them.

Birds: Great blue herons, kingfishers, blue-winged teals, wood ducks, mallards, Canada geese, sandpipers, bank swallows, owls, red-headed woodpeckers, pileated woodpeckers, flickers, magpies, cormorants, catbirds (call), bluejays (call), bald eagles, northern orioles.

Other vertebrates: Beavers, muskrats, painted turtles, snapping turtles, channel catfishes, northern pikes, walleyes, raccoons (tracks), red foxes, white-tailed deer.

Invertebrates. Flutedshell mussels, threeridge mussels, Wabash pigtoe mussels, pink heelsplitter mussels, white heelsplitter mussels, giant floater mussels, fatmucket mussels, plain pocketbook mussels, black sandshell mussels, pill clams (many trails), water scorpions.

Application to Life: Paddling an entire river system sets a long-term goal, useful in any endeavor. Besides gaining broad perspective from traveling a river's entire course, paddling one stroke at a time and totaling thousands to acquire that end, stands as a good lesson in persistence. So does devoting 9 years to paddling the entire Red Lake River. Paddling part of the first 78 miles against strong wind for 2 days gave me a further test of my persistence.

Chapter 7

Why Solo Travel?

Paddling solo may offer several benefits. Among them: living fully at the moment in a natural environment, developing self-reliance, and enjoying not having to compromise with a travel partner.

In Chapter 5, I mentioned devoting all your senses to your surroundings while on a C/K trip for maximum fulfillment. As you absorb what your senses tell you, you live completely and totally at the moment–a nice feeling. Your total being lies receptive to any challenge. Suppose you're relishing the comfort of a stream's current in relatively quiet water. This becomes punctured by the muffled roar of rough water ahead. Your senses go to alert status, and you stand up in your canoe for a preview of what lies ahead. In moments the muffled roar transforms to a solid, clear roar. You crank the canoe toward the right bank, quickly run through your options: run the rapids, line, or portage around them. A quick glance just before the last possible moment for a decision reveals too many upstream-pointing vees that signal numerous boulders. Now you whip your craft directly toward the right bank where you tie up.

You survey the rapids from a high cut bank, and decide to line the canoe. Half way through the lining, the rapids increase their volume, and you portage your craft and gear the rest of the way. As you look upstream, the rapids appear more menacing than when you viewed them from above. You played it safe, and made the right decision. With a partner, the result may have been the same. On the other hand, hurried and confused communication with him or her may have dulled and distracted your sensitivity to the rapids.

If you take a solo C/K trip that overtaxes your present ability, your senses may be overtaxed as well. But you likely will have fine tuned your living at the moment, and acquired the capability to react predictability to most any stimulus. In Chapter 11, I discuss two trips which I possibly should not have made. I wasn't in complete control of my watercraft at all times. But I lived at a lofty level during those journeys—and did I learn immeasurably about challenging water as well!

You can develop self-reliance while on solo water trips. Because only *you* must handle whatever weather and your surroundings can throw at you. As you paddle in and out of each predicament, like you stroke through each of life's predicaments, your list of accomplishments lengthens. Your self-confidence grows, along with your self-reliance. You learn to trust yourself, rather than having to rely on others. We can think of a progression: self-confidence>self-reliance>self-trust.

Traveling with others almost always requires some sort of compromise. This may be okay if you tend to be a compromising person. But sometimes you and your partner can't compromise.

"Should we camp above the island?"
"I'd rather camp below the island."

Compromise: You both camp on *the island.*
"Let's portage around the rapids."
"Disagree. Think we should line the canoe."
Compromise: You run *the rapids–together.*
"We could've gotten dumped back there."
"I know. But we were running late."

"Let's camp under the highway bridge."
"I'd rather not. Too close if someone spots us and decides to provoke us. Especially someone who might've been drinking. Let's camp a ways well below the bridge in some bushes."
No compromise. Your partner camps under the bridge, you camp well below in the bushes.

On longer trips with others, which I discuss in Chapter 8, you may find some solo time necessary. This becomes especially appropriate with a single partner, with whom you find yourself in contact at almost every moment. Such togetherness may prove disturbing at times. Park your tent some distance away to avoid your partner's snoring. Take a hike alone after dinner. At stops along the way, check out wildflowers in one direction while your partner goes in another to observe birds. With more than one other canoeist on a trip, sufficient diversity of personalities usually overcomes the need for solo time.

Some C/K trips simply might have to be taken alone. You might have a desirable water trip planned, but no one can accompany you at the time or duration that you've chosen. Or your agreed-upon companion may have taken ill. Or a substitute partner doesn't suit you.

If you haven't canoed or kayaked solo, give it a try. Just plan your journey well, take along back-up items like extra batteries and matches, and make your actions conservative and well thought-out.

When I travel alone, I'm not overly concerned over my safety on the water unless I'm on water chosen against my better judgment. I cover two such trips in Chapter 11. As for danger from wild animals, again not a primary concern. I worry more about being harassed or harmed by humans. If a stream possesses designated camp sites, especially with access roads to them, I rarely stay at such campsites. Instead, I choose my campsites above or below the designated ones. Maybe within 10 or 15 minutes of paddling time in case I must go to such sites because of an emergency. I worry, too, about leaving some crucial gear behind that I can't recover, such as a spare paddle or rain parka.

Now, I'll touch upon four of my easier solo canoe trips, and select the highlights. Three of these involve the Missouri River in northeastern Montana, the other the uppermost Mississippi River in northern Minnesota.

I took trip 53 on the Missouri from just below Ft. Peck Dam to Poplar in early August. Even though I put in at the left bank well below the dam, the lower part of the tail race presented choppy water that challenged me a bit. I felt my canoe twist and slip about, and had to apply a series of sweep strokes. The current remained relatively swift throughout the 94-mile trip as I averaged more than 4 mph. A generally southerly wind aided more than hindered my travel.

About 11 river miles below the dam, I came across a weathered, wooden ferry on the right bank. The tie-down cleats had also been fashioned of wood. Just below, I approached a ferry in use. A couple miles below the ferry, what appeared to be a highly weathered, wooden barge hugged the right bank. Seeing these relics from the past really made my day.

Tie-down cleat of a disused wooden ferry.

Because of troublesome small flies, I camped the first night at the upstream end of an island. This tactic has usually served me well in the past.

Interesting birds included Canada geese, pelicans, turkey vultures, and ring-necked pheasants. I estimated 60 geese congregated where the dam's spillway meets the river the first day. One group of turkey vultures numbered 16. I didn't see many pheasants but heard their numerous calls.

On a 2-day trip from southeast of Bainville, Montana to where U.S. Highway 85 crosses the river southwest of Williston, North Dakota (trip 48), I averaged about 4 mph. This, in spite of hard paddling at times because of wind. Canada geese and pelicans appeared here as on the Ft. Peck-Poplar trip. From my pup tent I heard many blowing and hoofbeat sounds by deer adjacent to my camp. I like such sounds, knowing other larger life moves about.

In a 12-mile stretch (trip 49) directly above where I put in for trip 48, I paddled against some of the strongest wind I've ever encountered. I calculated my average rate as only 2.5 mph. Logs in the bow provided insufficient weight for good trim, and I ended up paddling backward at times. Several dead calves and adult cattle floated in the river, likely having dropped in during a windy rainstorm. I attempted to help a rancher free a cow stuck in muddy sand on the right bank–a difficult job. At the put-in, where I estimated the river's width at 200 feet, I saw many white-tailed deer and pheasants and a muskrat. Canada geese also appeared on this trip.

A 3-day trip (13) in mid-August on the uppermost Mississippi River in northern Minnesota proved replete with worthwhile experiences while going solo. I paddled 26 miles from north-northwest of Lake Itasca to south of Wilton. The river generally trends northeast but numerous meanders cause the river to course in all directions. And the narrow river flows slowly; I averaged only 1.7 mph. Boulders the first couple miles scratched my canoe many times, and forced me to line the craft once. Water depth amounted to less than a foot in places. Then the bottom changed to sand. The first night I camped on high ground 10 minutes below Coffee Pot Landing, a designated campsite. I spotted an 18-inch northern pike in the clear water, and highbush cranberries with red fruit on the banks.

On the second day, boulders loomed in abundance above the Stumphges Rapids Forest Road. Common springs trickled along the banks. I always seek out springs for reliable fresh water. Below the Forest Road I found the first wild rice in profusion.

On this second day, a rare treat presented itself, and more meaningful because I received it alone. Five minutes below camp that morning, I attempted to photograph orange, dew-laden jewelweed blossoms. So intent on capturing an attractive close-up, I, at first, ignored a whirring sound close to me. Then, when repeated, I backed away slightly. A ruby-throated hummingbird probed its beak into a blossom of the same clump of plants I showed interest in–and no more than a foot from my head. I learned later that hummingbirds stand out as important pollinators of jewelweed, also called spotted touch-me-not because dry capsules shoot out their seeds when touched. This plant can be utilized as well as admired. Some rub on the stem juice to relieve itching from poison ivy.

On the last day, I experienced something never before or since. From the vicinity of Lake Monimin to the take-out at Pine Point Landing, I discovered much of the channel nearly choked by aquatic plants, especially pondweeds. And at three places in this stretch, the channel became *completely blocked* by reed grasses or cattails. What a feeling to look ahead and see no channel! I grabbed the canoe and manhandled it through the channel-blocking plants.

Application to Life: Learning to cope with solitude offers another benefit of solo travel. Some individuals consider themselves "people persons" and require constant contact with others. They might have difficulty in accomplishing anything on their own, and feel "lost" without companionship. Others, although they enjoy their association with friends, seek their own company at times. Having been raised as an only farm child, I've had an early and long experience with solitude. So, solo C/K trips have always seemed natural and comfortable to me. Regardless of which situation we normally favor, on occasion we find ourselves in solitary: You go to the dentist alone, you have surgery alone. You die alone.

Chapter 8

Longer Trips

I think of longer C/K trips as those lasting more than 3 days. These usually require some interpersonal adjustment, regardless of the number of watercraft involved. The adjustment may involve a period of testing.

One adjustment has to do with setting the pace of travel. If initially too high, some burn-out may settle in.

In a single canoe with two persons, probably the stern paddler usually sets the pace. If you find yourself in the bow, you might wonder if your effort matches that of your partner behind you. If he or she speeds up, should you as well, even though you're reluctant to do so?

In a second condition, assume your longer trip involves only you in one canoe and two others paddling tandem in another craft. Their combined effort consistently exceeds yours paddling solo, so they set the pace. As a consequence, they always outdistance you, and may flush animals before you've had the opportunity to see them. You mainly interact with them at lunch stops and at camp. Should you tell them that you simply cannot maintain their pace?

In two or more craft, each with two persons, the strongest pair will likely set the pace. The weaker paddler pairs may or may not concern themselves with lagging back. Each pair may consider itself separate and independent. Again, though, the strongest tandem will likely flush animals before others have the opportunity to observe them. Should you or your partner–if not the strongest paddlers–inform those who are, that you'd like to share what they experience up-front?

Three of my longer trips illustrate how experiences relate to trip duration: two on the Missouri and Yellowstone Rivers in north-central and northeastern Montana and the Mississippi in northeastern Minnesota.

The 6-day Missouri River trip (54), in mid- to late May, extended from Ft. Benton to where U.S. 191 crosses the river south of Landusky and the Little Rocky Mountains. Over a 150-mile stretch, the Missouri classifies as a National Wild and Scenic River.

This journey I took with Dale, a geology associate. Because we paddled in his canoe, I felt he had the edge on priority over our decisions. To his credit, though, he suggested we switch positions in the canoe often, which I favored.

Weather remained favorable: cool, partly to cloudy skies with only rare rain showers, but moderate to strong winds both in our favor and not.

The river stood at a high level with barely noticeable rapids. A fast current resulted in a paddling rate of 6.2 to 8.6 mph that averaged 6.9 mph. We attributed a common hissing sound to suspended sand grains in the highly turbulent water abrading the bottom of the canoe.

We navigated with old maps published by the Missouri River Commission in 1893. Hachures depicted variations in the terrain, not topographic contours. The maps displayed remarkable accuracy and relatively little change in the river's channel over a period of 170 years. We could identify many of the islands. River miles portrayed distances above Bismarck, North Dakota. We found plots of Lewis & Clark campsites of special interest. Those campsites, dated May 26 to June 12, 1805, downstream to upstream, encompass the distance of our trip. So the expedition passed through our stretch of the river roughly 1 to 3 weeks in the spring after us.

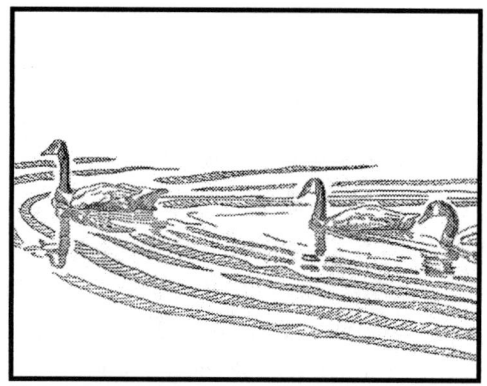

Canada geese in wake.

The White Cliffs Area below Coal Banks Landing and above the mouth of Arrow Creek took top billing as the most scenic segment of the river. Whitish sandstone especially contrasted with black lignite coal in the cut banks and cliffs.

Most conspicuous wildlife included the larger birds: Canada geese, great blue herons, pelicans, and cormorants. Canada geese, which we saw every day on bars or islands, topped the list. They most likely nested on the islands. On the second day we spotted seven yellowish young accompanied by three adult birds.

Our observations of Canada geese tied in nicely with those of the Lewis and Clark expedition. At the May 23, 1805 campsite, 6 miles below our take-out, Lewis wrote: "The Gees [sic] begin to lose the feathers of their wings and are unable to fly." At the expedition's May 26 campsite, about a mile below our camp 5, Clark wrote: "I saw . . . Geese of the common size & kind and a Small Species of geese, which differs considerably from the Common or Canadian Goose . . ." And, on June 12, about 6 miles below Ft. Benton, two other goose-related comments. Ordway wrote: "Saw . . . Geese & Goslings . . ." and Whitehouse said: ". . . in the River large flocks of Geese . . ." We felt good knowing, that 170 years after the expedition passed through on the Missouri, Canada geese continued to propagate their kind along the river.

A fascinating first for me at the time involved great blue heron nesting. On the first day below Ft. Benton, we discovered two of their rookeries or nesting grounds. The birds placed their nests in the upper parts of tall cottonwoods. This seemed strange, considering that these birds spend so much time in and near water. Between camp 5 and the mouth of the Judith River, a mile below, we marveled at another rookery in huge cottonwoods. I looked up at the impressive trees at camp and remarked: "Think of the weight. I worry about one of those cottonwoods coming down on us."

"Don't worry. These trees never come down," Dale assured me.

That night a loud crash awakened me in my pup tent as a cottonwood struck the ground–with no evident wind. I worried whether others seemed destined for descending to the earth in my vicinity.

We didn't see pelicans until the fifth day, at the downstream end of Council Island 3 ½ river miles below the mouth of the Judith River. Did this first sighting have something to do with the availability of their food?

Cormorants we sighted throughout the extent of the trip. But these birds could nowhere be considered common.

Special impressions of this trip include the calls of pheasants, geese, mourning doves, blackbirds, woodpeckers, owls, and other birds while in my pup tent in the morning or at night. No human sounds, just those of wildlife. In the morning, especially, before becoming fully awake, I'd wonder where I might be.

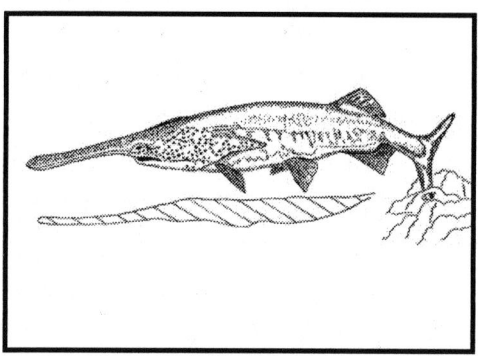

Paddlefish.

The only humans we witnessed on the river consisted of American History high school students in an 11-canoe flotilla from Eureka, Montana. They had made their clothing for this trip to simulate the dress of Lewis and Clark expedition days.

On the final full day, I felt rushed and exhausted from paddling, and would've preferred camping a few miles above the take-out at the U.S. Highway 191 bridge. But Dale pressed hard, believing the canoe outfitter at Ft. Benton would bring my partner's vehicle that day. The pick-up person, though, didn't arrive until the following day.

But the extra wait provided a bonus. Fishermen near the bridge brought in two paddlefish, one estimated at 4 ½ feet long and weighing 50 pounds, the other somewhat smaller. If unfamiliar with these creatures, also called "spoonbill catfish," one might imagine they're fitted with a canoe-paddle-like device for locomotion. Nothing could be farther from the truth. They have a paddle-shaped *snout,* which I learned later some believe might serve as a kind of antenna to detect water currents and bottom terrain. This odd snout, skeleton of cartilage instead of bone, and scaleless skin make them seem as creatures from the prehistoric past. Rather strange for fishes, paddlefish draw in large volumes of water from which to strain microscopic organisms on which they feed. As a result, fishermen can't use bait or lures but must snag the fish with large hooks.

The 5-day, 129-mile trip (58) on the Yellowstone River during the last week of May began at Terry, Montana and ended at the confluence of the Yellowstone and Missouri Rivers near the Ft. Buford Historic Site, North Dakota. Bill, a geology graduate, one of my advisees, and I paddled in my canoe. Dale, my partner on the 150-mile Missouri River trip below Ft.

Benton, shared his canoe with John, a geology professor colleague of mine.

We arrived late in Terry after a long drive from Grand Forks, North Dakota. So we opted to camp on the left bank of the river a mile northeast of town, and get an early start on the river in the morning.

Late that night, much commotion arose from raucous party-goers fortified with liquor. Apparently they saw us as strangers to their town whom they could harass a bit. Other members of my canoe party arose from their pup tents, but I remained in mine thinking that once they saw us, the longer they'd stay. One of the locals approached my tent and said, "Are you in there?" Pause. "How about if you come out? I'll give you a drink."

"No, thanks," I tried to be polite. "I don't drink."

A half hour later, they gave up on we "party-poopers" and left. With the quiet came many pheasant calls that lulled me to sleep.

The Yellowstone flowed slower than the Missouri, but we made a respectable rate of 4.6 to 5.9 mph over three segments of the Yellowstone. A strong southeast wind hindered us considerably the day we left Terry.

Cottonwoods, the most conspicuous trees, bore green seedpod clusters. Some released tufts of cottony seeds.

Paddlers in the other canoe pressed harder than did Bill and I, and seemed to favor being well ahead of us. We interacted with them mainly at campsites.

Canada geese and pelicans persisted throughout the trip. Other larger birds included great blue herons and rare cormorants. We also identified ovenbirds, mourning doves, and rose-breasted grosbeaks from their calls.

At Glendive, we learned of recent fires ahead, both along the river and in the hills and bluffs well away. Between our second camp, 3 miles below Glendive, and Intake, we saw what must have been thousands of acres of charred terrain. Burns seemed most conspicuous on the east side of the river. Fire clearly had no difficulty crossing the river with aid from strong westerly winds. We couldn't believe, at first, how green cottonwoods had burned as readily as the dry, dead trees. At one point, right on the river's bank, we came upon a farmstead. All displayed black except the house which had been saved by what we assumed must have been a valiant effort. The wildfires preceded us by only 2 days.

Once beyond the burns, a portage around the dam at Intake proved special. We saw a fisherman land a paddlefish estimated at 40 pounds. Not as large as the largest on the Missouri River trip, but, nevertheless, an eye-opener.

Our next to the last day on the river stood out as the most taxing–at 36 miles. And selection of a campsite, on the Montana-North Dakota border south of Fairview, sparked disagreement. Bill and I selected a high, grassy, left bank in a cow pasture. Dale and John camped on the downstream side of an island near the opposite, east bank. We believed the island site brushy and providing only a light breeze.

We paddled 30 miles to the take-out at the mouth of the Yellowstone, just a half mile east of the Ft. Buford Historic Site. To our surprise, the Yellowstone displayed much more turbid water than the Missouri.

This likely reflects, in part, the trapping of silt and clay by the Ft. Peck Reservoir.

A third longer trip (trip 22) took me to the upper Mississippi River in northeastern Minnesota. Malcolm, a biology graduate student, and his wife, Jenny, accompanied me. We put in at the east side of Grand Rapids, and took out where U.S. Highway 169 crosses the river north of Hassman. They paddled together in their canoe, I paddled alone in mine. On the 8-day journey in mid- to late May, we covered 85 miles for an average rate of only 2 1/4 mph. I attributed the low rate to a lower-than-normal river level and easterly and southeasterly winds that made paddling difficult at times. Light rain came often, and we paddled, at times, in it.

As for the other joint paddlers on the long Yellowstone River trip, Malcom and Jenny tended to remain well ahead. Their combined muscle power allowed them to continually outdistance me. We did, however, make some combined stops, and, of course, spent time together at camps.

Woods flanked the river through most of the trip. Deciduous trees–mainly silver maples, paper birches, ashes, elms, and basswoods–prevailed in the upper reaches of the journey, and coniferous woods became more frequent by the fifth day.

Because of Malcolm's greater proficiency with bird identification than I, we tallied more than 30 species for the journey. Among those seen along the Mississippi but not along the Missouri or Yellowstone, included bald eagles, hooded mergansers, nuthatches, ruffed grouse (both seen and heard their drumming), lesser yellowlegs, widgeons, phoebes, flickers, green herons, and blue jays. But, in like manner, we observed no Canada geese, pelicans, nor cormorants as on the two rivers in Montana.

Mammals seen along the Minnesota trip but not in Montana, included black bears, woodchucks, and mink.

At camp on the fifth day, Malcolm asked: "Did you see the mussels floating in the river?"

I looked at him in disbelief. "Mussels don't float. They live on the bottom."

"Well, we saw them floating. We'll try to pick them out tomorrow."

Biology student or not, I remained skeptical about his claim, which tugged at me during the night.

But the next day we saw, in fact, many floating mussels, and I made a collection. They floated both with and without their shells. My guess was that, upon death, gases of decomposition provided the means to float. But why did many die at once? I'll say more about this strange occurrence of mussels in Chapter 9.

I remained upbeat during this longer trip, and, what I could sense from my companions, so did they. But the seventh day came across as less appealing. The river seemed to have degenerated: more turbid than upstream, fewer bird species, no mammals, and only two floating mussels. We paddled in light rain much of the time. Our intended camp at Palisade seemed inhospitable—too open from town traffic, with doors off the toilets. We found it difficult finding another campsite away from town, roads, and dwellings. Finally, we set up camp below town—in the rain, and ate a cold dinner.

Light rain continued into the final morning, and we built a fire to dry out. Moderate to strong wind made paddling difficult at times. In view of what transpired the last 2 days, I felt this trip should be destined to end.

Application to Life: Setting the paddle pace can be likened to dating. The male usually sets the pace at which a relationship proceeds. If too rapid, the female may feel squeezed and backs off as if stung. If too slow, the female may sense the male's disinterest. If the female attempts to set the pace, the male feels he's lost control and will likely flee. Throughout the dating process, each tests the other for personal revelations. And if compromises come easily, the relationship solidifies.

Another analogy where setting the pace may threaten or disturb involves participating in a musical group—let's say with acoustical stringed instruments. Young players tend to play most tunes at a rapid speed—in large part to demonstrate that they have the capability to do so. Let's face it, "showing off" characterizes human nature. Older players may prefer their play at slower tempos, partly because their capability diminishes with age and also because slower play enhances the quality of their sound. If the musical pace conflict grows, young players split off to form their own fast-pace groups. So the rate at which you paddle or pick your guitar determines how you place in a stream or on the stage—as well as on the stage of life.

Chapter 9
Thrill of Discovery on the Water

We can expect natural world discoveries on the water with each paddle stroke and around each river bend. They may prove positive or negative. We, of course, seek attraction to the positive ones.

Everyone should feel the thrill and excitement of positive nature discovery, which can cause the adrenaline to race. Discoveries on the water vary with the person in terms of their relative significance. Finding a rare bird, mammal, or flower, or any of these where you least expect them, constitutes a kind of discovery. Some discoveries have a higher, and more meaningful status, such as those gleaned by scientists.

Scientists have a better-than-normal chance of experiencing major discoveries. Someone has said something like: "Luck happens to those who are well prepared." Their discoveries may be chance-induced, but scientists have been trained how to observe, reason, follow the scientific method. Imagine the rush of a paleontologist upon discovering a new species of dinosaur, or a biologist being blessed with finding a new mammal species when all the mammals seemingly had been tabulated. As a researcher of invertebrate fossils (extinct animals without backbones), I've been fortunate in discovering several species new to science. I recall the genuine thrill of each discovery. Above the thrill, though, necessitated the extra effort required to prove that I, indeed, had called attention to a truly new species.

I'll cover five of my discoveries on the water. A couple, at least, hinge on those scientific.

A 2-day canoe ride in northeastern Montana (trips 50 and 51) offered a highly unexpected discovery for my brother-in-law Frank and me. We covered 5 miles of the Big Muddy River due west of Culbertson and 26 miles of the Missouri River above and below town. A dead pelican at the mouth of the Big Muddy struck me as a bad omen. But downstream we picked up on Canada geese, some, presumably, nesting pairs. Then, below an island on the outside of a meander, 2 ½ miles south of Culbertson, something different caught my eye in the right cut bank. I yelled to Frank : "Put on the breaks. Paddle backward!" The high water and swift current made our reversed motion difficult. But finally we maneuvered to the feature in question. I leaped out of the canoe, tied it up with the rear painter. In a scramble part way up the cut bank, I approached what had caught my eye: a single horn core of a bison skull! Lady Luck surely backed me this time. The 8-inch horn core barely protruded from the cut bank, about 4 feet below the floodplain. Frank looked up from the canoe, smiled broadly.

We only had two hunting knives to serve as excavating tools. After some work, we found the skull lying upside down in thinly-layered clay, silt, and sand. We eventually freed the skull from its place of entombment, and recovered the lower jaws as well. Upon examining the cut bank several feet away, we discovered a bonus: a complete half of an elk antler!

The antler seemed positioned at about the same level in the cut bank as the bison skull.

After freeing the elk antler, we sat for a rest. I looked at Frank. "How are we going to get these bones back home? Canoe's full. No room."

"Best bet," Frank replied, "is to drag them up to the level ground above us, and hide them in the bushes. We'll mark the spot, and come back for them with my vehicle tomorrow."

Excavating a bison skull (large arrow) and an elk antler (small arrow) in a cut bank of the Missouri River near Culbertson, Montana.

The skull, packed with sediment, proved heavy for both of us. But we loaded it and all the bones in Frank's vehicle. At his place, I spent a couple hours flushing out sediment with a water hose. Later, I varnished the skull to preserve it.

A natural question: How old were the bones? Short of having the bones dated, we had no idea. When elk were last known in northeastern Montana would have given a minimum age.

The bone discovery overshadowed other experiences on this trip: Hearing coyotes from our pup tents at night. Seeing three dead cattle floating in the river. Seeing a shaggy mane mushroom growing from cow droppings. Seeing much poison ivy with leaves just forming, and later developing a rash of watery blisters.

Ken, a geology graduate student, and I followed a quest for much older fossils while canoeing on the Pembina River west and north of Walhalla, North Dakota (trip 43). He pursued a master's thesis under my direction on fossils from the 90-million-year-old Carlile Formation, the oldest rock exposed in the state. This formation, of dark gray to black shale, represents an offshore mud laid down in a seaway that covered several states. We expected to find exposures of this shale in the deepest parts of the Pembina River Gorge. Not a gorge, as those in the American Southwest, but a relatively deep valley.

We canoed about 28 miles, from where Manitoba Provincial Road 201 crosses the river to Walhalla. Taking the trip during the third week in June proved unwise. A low water level necessitated our lining my canoe around rapids with numerous rocks–13 times! And within the last 3 miles we had difficulty navigating around sand and gravel bars and tree snags. But we made a paddling rate of about 4 mph in spite of the low water.

About 1 ½ hours below the put-in, we spotted a bison skull in a cut bank. But incomplete, unlike the skull on the Missouri River south of Culbertson, Montana, we let it be.

In the end, the low water, in spite of making travel difficult, turned fortunate for us. A dozen miles up river from Walhalla, we stopped at a 75-foot exposure of Carlile shale for a look. In what geologists call "concretions," rock hard masses of shale cemented with limy mineral matter, we found several fossils, just a foot or two above water level. If we had come down the river at a slightly higher level, we would have completely missed the fossils.

In the concretions, we found two kinds of small clams, a snail, and an animal distantly related to the living chambered nautilus. But the highlight of our fossil discovery? A fossil clam more than 13 inches across. We both felt giddy from the discovery. Ken collected all the fossils, which became part of his thesis.

I discuss three coastal sea kayak trips in Chapter 10. Two of these involve discoveries while traveling the waters of the San Juan Islands, Washington.

While on a 6-day journey in the waters of Rosario Strait (trip 77), my group of sea kayakers camped two nights at Matia Island. This allowed us to completely encircle Sucia Island one day. At the south end, we stopped at Fossil Bay–aptly named as I soon realized. Rock layers here tilt to the northeast, not flat-lying like the Carlile Formation along the Pembina River. Hoping the group of kayakers would remain here a reasonable time, I scrambled over many of the rock layers looking for fossils. I saw nothing in the sandstone and conglomerate (lithified gravel). But in gray mudstone at the southwest edge of the bay, fossils occurred in abundance: mostly clams, but also snails, tusk shells, and shells of animals distantly related to the living chambered nautilus. Some of the fossils looked generally similar to those Ken and I found on the Pembina River, and they occurred in similar-appearing rocks. The ages of the two groups of fossils, too, seemed to be roughly the same.

I shared my excitement over the fossil find with other members of my kayak group. They ooh-ed and ahh-ed over the well-preserved fossils, and seemed to mostly accept my explanations about their identity. To date, this event remains my sole opportunity at collecting fossils from a sea kayak while in marine waters.

A second discovery took place while paddling a sea kayak in the waters of the San Juan Islands, this time along Haro Strait. On the last day of a 4-day trip (trip 78), a group of 9 of us stopped at Yellow Island on the way back to San Juan Island. In shallow water I could see large red sea urchins and orange sea cucumbers, among other creatures. Then, I began turning over flat boulders exposed at low tide, but not sure why. In time, I discovered two, small brachiopods attached to the underside of one boulder. Hooray! I thought. I had studied numerous fossil brachiopods—and named a few new species—but had never seen a live one. Because Yellow Island is owned by The Nature Conservancy, I didn't collect specimens. Brachiopods resemble clams in having two parts to their shells but internally they appear quite different. They reached their peak of most species roughly 400 million years ago, and today relatively few species exist. Today, too, brachiopods tend to favor deeper waters than those of the past.

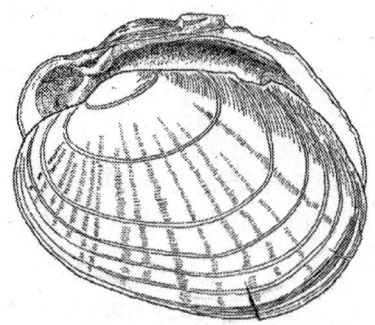

A plain pocketbook mussel found floating in the Mississippi River near Libby, Minnesota. The mussel measures about 3 ½ inches across.

In Chapter 8, I mentioned finding floating mussels in the Mississippi River while on an extended canoe trip in northeastern Minnesota. Scepticism surfaced from me at first when Malcolm, a biology graduate student, prepared to point them out to me in the vicinity of Libby. But his observation, of course, proved correct. Hooked on this unusual occurrence, I collected 14 shells of the fatmucket mussel and one of the plain pocketbook. The largest fatmucket measured just under 3 inches long and weighed seven-tenths of an ounce. The plain pocketbook measured about 3 1/2 inches long and weighed about 1 ½ ounces. The mussels apparently floated because of trapped gases in decomposing flesh.

River discharge data near Libby showed the lowest value for May one day before we saw the first floating mussels. Then, the discharge rose for six consecutive days. I postulated that the mussels died upon exposure to the air upon a rapidly falling water level. Their flesh decomposed with trapping of the resulting gases. Rapid rising water levels loosened the shells by wave and current action, and the smaller shells floated to the surface.

I believed these floating mussels could warrant as a minor scientific discovery, of greater significance than other so-called discoveries mentioned in this chapter. A published account, therefore, appeared in 2001: "Cvancara, Alan M., Floating mussels in the upper Mississippi River, Minnesota and their implications for dispersal in paleontology and archeology," *Central Plains Archeology*, v. 8, no. 1, pages 143-148.

Application to Life: Interpersonal discoveries, like on-the-water, natural world discoveries, may similarly appear at each temporal bend in our lives. And they may be positive or negative. A member of the opposite sex may inform you of his or her love, or your spouse may reinforce that love as well. Or, the woman or man friend or spouse may bid you sayonara. Negative discoveries, especially, may drop into our lives when we least expect them.

Chapter 10
Protected Oceanic Sea Kayaking

Born and mostly bound to the heart of the North American continent–a point south of Rugby, North Dakota locates the exact center–I felt compelled to sample coastal sea kayaking. My test of coastal waters took place on three July trips, one in British Columbia, the others in the waters of the San Juan Islands, Washington. The crucial variable, as compared to large-lake kayaking, boils down to tides. You travel with tide tables, and paddle with the tides, not against them.

Johnstone Strait, British Columbia

What really attracted me to the Johnstone Strait area (trip 76), near the northwestern tip of Vancouver Island, lay the prospect of sighting killer whales. And Johnstone Strait had been considered as a killer whale "hot spot." My group, led by Dean and his companion, Connie, both highly knowledgeable, put in our two-holer kayaks at Telegraph Cove, east of Port McNeill.

Once on the water, Dean announced a cautionary remark about killer whales. "If you suspect killer whales nearby, rap your hand against the kayak. The sound waves give the animals something to echolocate on. The chances of killer whales attacking you is essentially nil. But not knowing if you are above them, they might dump you when they surface."

We progressed slowly on our shakedown cruise, paddled 7 miles in 2 ½ hours. We camped on the south edge of Johnstone Strait just west of the mouth of Kaikash Creek.

Killer whales, a presumed male on the left, with the taller dorsal fin, and a female on the right. The two swim to the right as evidenced by a light "saddle patch" at the rear of the dorsal fin, and a steeper slope to the rear edge of the fin.

Just offshore from camp, we picked up our first killer whales, also called orcas or blackfish. We saw three "pods," or identifiable groups, that averaged about eight per pod. Imagine how I felt, a landlubber, witnessing these largest of dolphins in the wild. They blew frequently, their sound like that of air rushing and echoing through a tube. Occasionally they "breached" or jumped out of the water and landed on their side, stomach, or back. I marveled at their ebony bodies and large dorsal fins. They also displayed white bellies, white spots above their eyes, and a light "saddle patch" behind the fin.

Besides the orcas, two other creatures confirmed our proximity to marine waters: a seal and marbled murrelets, in brown-backed, summer plumage. Common bald eagles, though, maintained my inland tie.

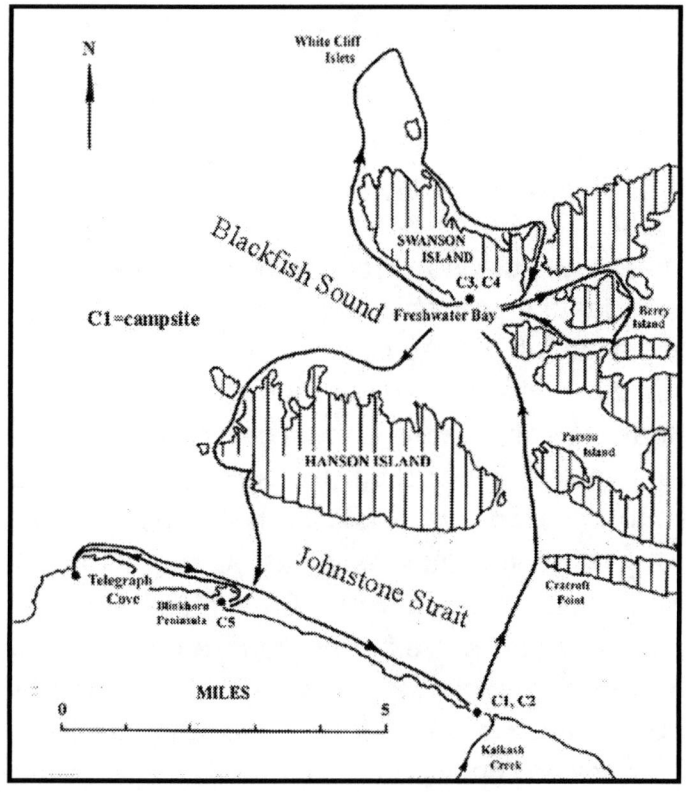

Map of Johnstone Strait and vicinity, showing the route traveled and campsites. Port McNeill lies to the left or west.

While eating dinner, a Dutch cruise ship passed from Blackfish Sound and disappeared to the right or southeast of us. I felt so inconspicuous in the presence of such a huge, brightly-lit vessel.

During the night and early the following morning, I heard orcas blow while tucked away in my pup tent. At the first blow, I asked, "Where am I?" Then I gave thanks for being there and nowhere else.

The strong west-northwest wind of our initial day forged on to the next. Dean explained: "I know you're all anxious to travel, but it's too risky to cross Johnstone Strait in this wind. Find something to do today. We'll get up at 4 a.m., and be on the water by 5 or so. Maybe we can avoid the choppy water of the past 2 days. Don't worry. We'll see plenty before this trip's over."

Heavy Johnstone Strait traffic continued. Besides another large cruise ship and smaller watercraft, a tug pulling a log raft passed by our camp.

In the morning, we began paddling at 5 a.m. in darkness. Dean checked his large compass mounted just in front of his cockpit and said, "All of you stay close to me. Don't want to lose anyone out here in the dark." We headed northerly past Cracroft Point and Parson Island into Blackfish Sound and Freshwater Bay at the southeast edge of Swanson Island. Fog, a continued west-northwest wind, and a later drizzle all made our crossing, which took 2 ½ hours, difficult.

We came upon two orca pods, one with six animals, the other with three. So eerie their blows seemed–issuing from the fog.

A magical moment occurred just as we crossed Johnstone Strait and paused our paddling. The smaller pod loomed before us, and the largest animal displayed a missing rear part of the dorsal fin–likely from a bite.

Within a few seconds, the fog consumed the pod, and testimony of an orca battle. A slow blink or a resting of the eyes and we would have lost this cherished event.

With our camp established at Freshwater Bay, we paddled around Berry Island. At a few places, we saw what, at first, resembled white beaches above high tide. These, however, came to pass as eroded, Indian shell middens. Up close, we recognized expectable shells of butter clams, littleneck clams, and gaper clams. But the large acorn barnacles, two or more inches high, which made up most of the middens, caught my eye. I had never seen any of such size on the California, Oregon, and Washington coasts. I surmised that Indians could have harvested the barnacles more easily than the clams, and tested the thought. With a rock that fit comfortably in my hand, I whopped a couple of barnacles off rock surfaces, each with a single blow.

Dean and Connie prepared fine meals, often incorporating wild ingredients. The rest of us shared in the cleanup. I especially favored bull kelp and creamed shrimp. They separated several blades of bull kelp from the float and cut them into narrow strips, which resembled spaghetti after boiling. The creamed shrimp made a fine sauce for the bull kelp. Dean and Connie had no difficulty in keeping food from spoiling. Hatch-covered compartments in the kayaks served as refrigerators because of water temperatures in the 40s.

Our stomachs satisfied with bull kelp and shrimp, we turned our conversation to orcas. Someone asked Dean: "How do you distinguish the males from the females?"

"That's pretty easy if the animals are mature. Mature males have larger dorsal fins–up to 6 feet high. My researcher friends tell me, though, that it's virtually impossible to tell immature males and non-breeding females," replied Dean.

"What do they eat?" asked another voice.

"They're not interested in us, of course. During the summer months, they prefer salmon. They also take other fish, porpoises, seals, sea lions, and minke whales. I've even heard of a cormorant found in a dead orca."

"I'm really interested in their behavior," asked still another voice. "Besides the breaching we saw on the first day, what else do they do?"

"Quite a bit, besides foraging for food. 'Spyhopping' is an interesting behavior. If curious about their surroundings or an approaching boat, they rear their heads out of the water for a look-see. Another antic is 'beach rubbing,' where they rub their bodies against smooth pebbles along the shore. My researcher friends say beach rubbing may remove algae or dry skin, or maybe it just feels good."

"Anything else?" the third voice persisted.

"Two others are 'tail-lobbing' and 'flipper-lobbing.' In tail-lobbing, the orca lies on its back or stomach at the surface. It lifts its tail flukes in the air and slams them down on the surface. In flipper-lobbing, the orca lies on its side and flaps its flipper against the water's surface. Both of these behaviors often create a loud noise at the surface. Some say they produce an underwater signal."

Rain spattered during the night and part of the morning. Camped just above high tide line, I first heard lapping waves in the morning. Then, another sound, but much feebler. I knew it, but couldn't identify it at first in my dazed state. Ah, yes, hummingbird wing beats! My mind skipped briefly to the upper Mississippi River in northern Minnesota where I experienced the same sound while photographing jewelweed blossoms.

We paddled northerly along the west coast of Swanson Island to White Cliff Islets. Terrain at the islets had clearly been molded by glaciers encroaching from the east. Tidal pools harbored black and lined chitons, and painted tealia and white-spotted tealia sea anemones. Just below low tide, starfish abounded, accompanied by orange sea cucumbers. As on the first day, we sighted many bald eagles. On the return near Round Islet, a minke whale passed us, recognized, in part, by its short dorsal fin.

The second evening at Freshwater Bay, Dean asked me: "Want to come along while I try to catch a fish for dinner? You can control the kayak while I fish."

"Sure," I replied. "Where are we headed?"

"We'll strike out west a ways into Blackfish Sound."

Dean caught no fish. But blessed with a fortunate stroke, we saw three orcas come within our vision, maybe half a mile away. Two veered off, but the third maintained its course toward us. Dean stowed his fishing rod.

"Here," said Dean, as he handed me headphones and lowered a hydrophone into the water. He either had considerable experience with orcas or luck rode our shoulders. The orca now closer still, Dean said softly: "Must be a mature bull coming at us. Dorsal fin's a good 6 feet high."

When within 40 feet of us, the bull dove. I tuned in the hydrophone to distinguish high-pitched clicks of echolocation, whines, and other vocalizations that Dean later attempted to explain to me.

Rain during the night ushered fog in the early morning: an essential repeat of the night and morning before. In disbelief in my pup tent, I thought I had been dreaming. But no, I heard the same sounds repeated from the previous morning–lapping waves and hummingbird wing beats. What had I done right to deserve such a moment again?

At breakfast, a kayaking couple in separate kayaks from Victoria stopped by while on a multi-day trip. They left us chinook salmon that they had caught the night before. How much fresher can you have your fish? Their equipment and demeanor revealed their being well accustomed to sea kayak travel. They had fashioned fishing rod holders, set and sealed into the tops of their kayaks, for a handy reach from paddle to fishing rod.

As we broke camp, I attempted to dismantle the campfire. In the rush, I grabbed a piece of firewood that retained hot coals on the underside. Immersing my hand in cold Freshwater Bay water quelled the burning pain. Connie, a nurse, applied a salve, which allowed me to paddle directly without holding up the rest.

We paddled across Blackfish Sound along the northwest and west sides of Hanson Island and rested after 2 hours at a small cove east of Weynton Island. Our course took us directly south across Johnstone Strait to Blinkhorn Peninsula in 45 minutes: an easy crossing compared with the 2 ½-hour battle 2 days before.

We set up camp on the south or protected side of Blinkhorn Peninsula, and marveled at several cruise ships on nocturnal passages from Blackfish Sound.

We awoke to a clear morning and little wind. Three bald eagles graced our camp. On the easy, 1-hour paddle to Telegraph Cove, we came upon another minke whale, a fitting flourish to a fine adventure.

Rosario Strait, Washington

Now let's skip to the southeastern tip of Vancouver Island, where the nearby San Juan Islands form a loose cluster tucked between the cities of Victoria, B.C. and Anacortes, Washington. Rosario Strait, the setting for trip 77, flanks the eastern side of the islands.

Six kayakers paddled three double kayaks and Carl, outfitter-leader in his 30s, and I paddled single kayaks on this 6-day trip. We left Sunset Beach in Anacortes on a flood tide and an 8-knot, southerly wind—an easy embark.

A 7 ½- mile paddle took us to Pelican Beach at the north end of Cypress Island, our first camp. Rhinoceros auklets, pigeon guillemots, and harbor seals clearly told us of our travel in marine waters. From camp, we hiked more than a mile to Eagle Cliff through woods of Douglas fir, hemlock, cedar, and alder—so dense as to virtually lack an understory. The cliff of dark-colored basalt, a rock once molten, displayed a pillow structure that revealed its emplacement in water. At 800 feet above sea level, we could make out many islands: Orcas, Shaw, San Juan, Vancouver, and Lummi.

After dinner, someone asked Carl: "What's that thick book you're reading?"

"Tide tables. You don't travel anywhere without them."

"Yeah?"

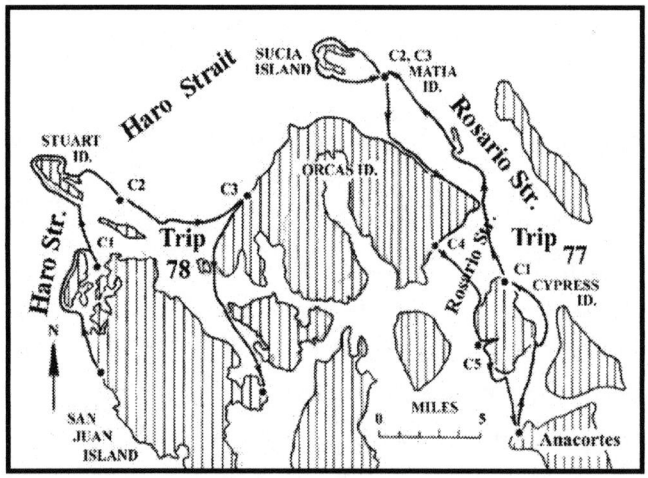

Map of the San Juan Islands showing the routes of trips 77 and 78 and campsites. Trip 77 associates with Rosario Strait, trip 78 with Haro Strait.

"Imagine the San Juans as giant boulders in a giant stream that periodically reverses its flow direction. During flood tide, tidal currents flow *north*; and during ebb tide, they flow *south*. This is the basic pattern. But confusing eddies and flow reversals take place where tidal currents flow close to the islands. The tide tables explain many of these exceptions, but not all. The doubtful ones come with travel experience out here. I wouldn't recommend kayaking alone in the San Juans until you've gained some of that experience."

In the morning, we set out past Lawrence Point at the eastern tip of Orcas Island, between Barnes and Clark Islands, and on to Matia Island, where we camped at Rolfe Cove. This segment required 3 ½ hours of paddling. Seals abounded in the vicinity of Barnes and Clark Islands. Two other coastal birds appeared: marbled murrelets and black oystercatchers.

Carl demonstrated his proficiency in the Eskimo roll. He could easily execute two or three in succession. No one else, however, attempted the maneuver in the cold water.

We settled into a routine with meals. Carl prepared the basic meal, while others prepared salads. All of us, except Carl, took turns at washing dishes and kettles.

On our second day camped at Matia, we spent the day paddling around Sucia Island, with stops at Ewing Cove, Sucia Cove, and Fossil Bay. I've already mentioned the discovery of fossils at Fossil Bay in Chapter 9.

The next day proved eventful in more ways than one. We had a rough 1-hour crossing over part of Rosario Strait, heading due south from Matia to Orcas Island, and using Mt. Constitution as a guide. A localized head wind slid down the steep slopes of Mt. Constitution, and we also experienced resistance from tidal currents at times.

"Stay together!" Carl hollered at us several times. "For Christ's sake, how can I watch all of you when you keep drifting apart!" Staying together proved a bit difficult under the trying circumstances. In spite of the hard paddling, we registered a whale blowing during the crossing, but at a distance too far to identify. Some in the group also sighted sea otters. As we approached

Lawrence Point, a stiff southeastern head wind made paddling even more difficult.

A rest stop taught me about the unexpected. We pulled our kayaks up a short distance on a smooth pebble beach. As we snacked and Carl chastised us further for not sticking together, one of the kayaks began to slide toward the sea on the bed of smooth pebbles. I ran to the craft and rescued it before it slid all the way into the water, which topped my rubber boots. Carl showed no immediate concern. But I pulled my kayak higher up on the beach.

We camped on the east side of Doe Island at the east edge of Orcas Island and southwest of Lawrence Point. Before reaching camp, a great blue heron perched on a mass of bull kelp, which the bird used as a handy fishing platform.

After setting up my pup tent, I rested and thought about the extremely hard 10 miles from Matia: *HAVE I EVER FELT SUCH ACHING SHOULDERS FROM PADDLING? Probably not. Not even on the 68-mile, head-wind paddle on the Red Lake River, Minnesota between its source and Thief River Falls.*

Sensing our reluctance toward dinner because of fatigue, Carl announced: "I'm sure you're all beat from today's paddle. But I've got a surprise for you. There's a resort just northwest of camp, and they've got a hot tub." A loud cheer punctured the quieting evening.

After showering and leaving my clothes at the shower stalls, I headed up the hill to the outdoor hot tub. A sign at the hot tub caused me to hesitate: SWIMSUITS OPTIONAL. Carl and a shapely 20-something from our group occupied one end of the tub, a couple in their 50s the other. Neither of the four considered wearing tub attire as an option. The shapely 20-something provided a treat for weary eyes and body, but, distinctly seen in the clear water, the 50-ish female did not. She displayed bulges where they should not be. And her smoking cigarettes while in the tub did not add to the image. As for the men, I could imagine their looking better with pubic areas covered.

Carl apparently thought it prudent to make our fifth day an easy one after the hard haul the day before. We paddled on an ebb tide 5 miles southeast to Strawberry Island, a half mile west of Cypress Island. Two tug-pulled barges passed before us. Twice as fast as our kayaks—making 6 knots versus our 3—we learned early never to attempt crossing in front of a moving barge.

I pitched my pup tent on a small grassy platform at the top of a sea cliff: a perfect spot with a wide expanse of the protected sea. Carl recommended this spot when I asked him for the most private site. I looked forward to some solitude after the previous day's arduous paddle amidst Carl's officious prodding. Masses of bull kelp floated below me.

We really understood the meaning of tidal currents while standing at the southern tip of Strawberry Island during flood tide. The currents would impinge from the south, then split to pass on both sides. They closely resembled the riffles and rapids you might see in a stream.

I had hoped for more time to witness invertebrate animals in shallow water from the kayak. But I did revel in the special sighting of orange sea cucumbers, and large, red sea urchins.

Heavy fog enshrouded us the final morning, and we paddled in fog along the western shoreline of

Cypress Island, and around Reef Point. We lunched nearby while waiting for the fog to lift. Carl became impatient, so we paddled the final 2½ miles across the Bellingham Channel to Sunset Beach–partly in a driving rain and fog.

I felt apprehension over our course that took us across a major ferry lane, and shuddered to imagine how we'd fare should a ferry suddenly loom before us. The ferry's captain most likely wouldn't see us–minute slivers on the indistinct water–and we wouldn't respond quickly enough to avoid collision.

My overall impressions of trip 77? 1. Carl, our guide, demonstrated knowledgeability and generally caution and good judgment for the safety of the group. His eagerness to cross Bellingham Channel in rain and fog stands as an exception. 2. When the going got rough, or group members didn't follow instructions, he barked orders or reprimands. 3. Paddling a single kayak, I lagged behind on occasion. Did others, all younger than me, stand out as stronger paddlers? Or could my craft have been more heavily loaded? 4. I did not favor traveling with a group, although this offers a greater margin of safety. More sea kayaking experience would be wise before attempting a trip in the San Juans alone.

Haro Strait, Washington

Haro Strait flanks the western side of the San Juan Islands as does Rosario Strait on the eastern side. Trip 78 followed part of Haro Strait. I paddled with a group of eight adults and a teenage girl in four kayaks. Again, as for the other two trips in coastal waters, I opted for July, a time with little chance of rain.

From our put-in at San Juan County Park on the west side of San Juan Island, we paddled past the west side of Henry Island and around McCracken Point to Posey Island, our first camp. At one point we watched a fishing boat take in a purse seine with maybe 100 salmon. I believed that we approached too closely, and expected the captain to scold us for interfering with the fishing boat's haul. But Odin, our leader, showed no sign of backing off. With restraint, the captain picked up a 2-foot silver salmon and tossed it to Odin. "Here, try this," he shouted. Maybe he presented the offering to get rid of us. Odin popped the fish into a cool, hatched compartment where it would keep until evening, and we paddled away.

Besides the coastal rhinoceros auklets and pigeon guillemots that we enjoyed on trip 77, I added harlequin ducks to my bird list. Bald eagles persisted as well. But a sobering sight countered the pleasant ones: a floating deer fawn. We often need reminding of the lives the sea claims.

At camp, someone recovered a rusting, wire grill. After abrasion-cleaning in sand, Odin cooked our silver salmon over hot coals. I couldn't believe how good ultra-fresh salmon might be!

After dinner, we paddled the short distance to Roche (pronounced ROACH) Harbor, now a tourist town. At one time the town supported a lime industry.

I awoke in the morning to six seals just offshore from my tent. We paddled the Posey Island-Stuart Island stretch in 50 minutes. River otter frolicked among bull kelp at the southern edge of Stuart Island.

We worked our way around Turn Point, and camped on Johns Island.

Odin taught us how to set up our pup tents on a pebble gravel beach, a really useful technique. Instead of attempting to use tent stakes, which proved useless, we tied our tent lines to pieces of driftwood, and buried them in the gravel. If done right, the anchoring pieces of driftwood allowed sufficient tightening of the tent lines.

One thing, though, bothered me about camping a few yards from the sea's edge and only about two vertical feet above the high-water mark. A tsunami slamming into our beach camp would wipe us all away.

A couple invertebrates made this day special: whitish jellyfish and, at minus low tide, orange sea cucumbers with conspicuous orange tentacles. I also observed many of the same kind of jellyfish attached to the salmon fisherman's net the day before.

Two paddlers in a double kayak lagged way behind the rest of us, arousing Odin's concern. But he didn't overtly reprimand them as Dean did on the Rosario Strait trip,

We broke camp for Flattop Island and a crossing of President Channel to the northwest edge of Orcas Island, due west of Turtleback Mountain and camp 3. Several seals and a few bald eagles kept our interest along the way. At camp 3, I collected three kinds of limpet snails from rock ledges. I guessed that gulls had dropped the limpets here to feed on them

Two kayakers in my group paddled near camp after sundown. They returned excited about many flashing lights in the water from some unknown organisms.

"Yeah," Odin pointed out, "biologists call this 'bioluminescence.'"

Odin, in his 30s, seemed to become more friendly with the teenage girl as the trip wore on: setting up her tent, going on hikes with her. At one point, he shared his pipe with her at the campfire. I wondered whether he had gone beyond the bounds of his guiding duties.

On our final day, we paddled by Jones Island to Yellow Island and across San Juan Channel to San Juan Island near Friday Harbor. I mentioned finding living brachiopods on The Nature Conservancy's Yellow Island as one of my on-the-water-discoveries in Chapter 9.

My overall impressions of trip 78? 1. It ranks lowest of my three coastal oceanic trips, likely because of the trip leader's handling of it. Besides his fraternizing with a teenage girl, he seemed to economize with food. Example: Preparing hamburgers from soybeans. And when we landed at the take-out point, the ebb tide forced us to drag kayaks and lug gear across an extensive, muddy tidal flat. Maybe the take-out could have been timed during a flood tide. 2. I still didn't like kayaking with a group, having to make compromises. But, even after three trips, I believed my experience with coastal sea kayaking remained insufficient for going it solo.

Application to Life: Coastal oceanic sea kayaking involves danger from ferries, cruise ships, and log rafts, and the ever-present tides. Confrontations in life involve financial insecurity, interpersonal relationships, and unexpected deaths.

Chapter 11

C/K Trips That Preview as Reckless

Waters for C/K trips can group into three categories: clearly runnable, clearly unrunnable, and questionably runnable. The third category often becomes difficult to identify, and reduces margins of safety. Two inner voices give contrary advice. One says: "Go ahead. You can do it. Accept the challenge. Don't be a wimp." The other argues: "This water's too fast for you. And, with too many rapids. You want to hurt yourself–or die? Is this trip worth the risk?"

You might paddle questionably runnable water for the sake of acquiring more experience. In time, this added experience may place questionably runnable water into the clearly runnable category.

I've singled out two solo trips identified as questionably runnable at the time I took them. I made a reckless "go" decision for each, and took unnecessary risks. Had these not been solo trips, they likely would have been identified as "runnable."

Yellowstone River, Montana: Big Timber to Laurel

Two days before this trip (59), son Mark and I canoed 28 miles of the Yellowstone downstream from Yellowstone National Park (trip 60), and took out below

Emigrant, Montana. Because of heavy runoff in mid-June, we averaged a paddling rate of 8 mph. I could hear sand abrading the bottom of the aluminum canoe, as I also had experienced on the Missouri below Ft. Benton (trip 54). We discovered that, at times, light rain made it difficult seeing submerged boulders, which could snag us and threaten a capsize.

Upon sizing up the swift river at Livingston, I concluded the idea of a put-in there as foolhardy. Ella said: "After seeing the river several times from the road, I can't believe you'd even stop and check on it here in town. I think you should give up more trips on this river."

Ella usually didn't tell me what to do when it came to canoeing. Although I paid heed to what she said, I wasn't ready to give up on another go with the Yellowstone.

At Big Timber, I took another serious look at the river. It was high and fast, and I, of course, didn't know what lay ahead.

Ella asked, "You're not going to run the river from here, are you?"

"I've been thinking about it." The challenge of the river overcame my better judgment. "Yeah, I'm going to take it to Laurel. You can pick me up there. Maybe about mid-afternoon or so."

"I wish you wouldn't do this," Ella replied. "Should something happen to you, I don't know what I'd do."

"I think I'll be all right," I said with little conviction, and changed the subject. "You'll be staying overnight at Don's and Alice's place, even though they'll be gone?" On trip 34, Alice, during her pregnancy, felt the frequent need to urinate in a can while we canoed with her and Don on the Red Lake River, as mentioned in Chapter 6.

"That's the plan. They'll be on vacation." She handed me a slip of paper with a telephone number. "Give me a call when you reach Laurel–*if* you reach Laurel."

Grabbed by the abrupt swiftness of the river, I soon wished it would slow. I canoed the 73 miles between Big Timber and Laurel in 10 ½ hours of paddling time for an average rate of 7 mph. As on the Yellowstone below Yellowstone National Park and the Missouri below Ft. Benton, I often heard suspended sand abrading the bottom of the canoe. I didn't lean into the paddle much, just mostly steered and guided the canoe away from rapids where possible. Standing waves and rapids showed up everywhere, with waves up to 3 feet high. A light westerly wind, however, offered some assistance.

I took two precautions. One, I trailed a 25-foot rope knotted at intervals; I hoped to grab the rope should I get dumped, so as not to be separated from the canoe. The other, I knelt in the bottom of my craft at times to lower the center of gravity and make it more stable.

Rapids gave me most difficulty at the bridge in Columbus and below Columbus where I thought it certain that I would capsize. At one point the river split at an island. I chose the left divided channel. When the right channel joined the left one, the high waves at the downstream end of the island nearly swamped me. Water slapped into the canoe, testimony to the height of the waves.

Besides the challenging rapids and waves, I had another nemesis: tree trunks lying horizontally against cut banks with water flowing beneath them. Ample space beneath the tree trunks could trap a canoe and its paddler. Most of the time, I tried to position myself close to the center of the channel so as not to be swept under fallen trees.

In spite of the rather hectic ride, I squeezed in a few nature observations. Trees on the dry hills seemed to be mostly ponderosa pines and Rocky Mountain junipers; those along the river, mostly narrow-leaved and plains cottonwoods and willows. Birds included some of the standards: Canada geese, cormorants, great blue herons, mallards, blue-winged teals, owls (call), sandpipers, and bank and cliff swallows.

At the take-out, Ella didn't ask me about the trip. And I thought it fitting not to discuss it. I was most thankful at having arrived in Laurel safely.

Apostle Islands, Wisconsin

The Apostle Islands, at the southwestern edge of Lake Superior, cluster off the Bayfield Peninsula in northwestern Wisconsin. Twenty of the 22 islands make up most of the Apostle Islands National Lakeshore.

The Apostle Islands bear similarities to the San Juan Islands in coastal Washington. Both group into similar-sized clusters: the Apostles about 22 by 27 miles, the San Juans about 25 by 30 miles. The Apostle cluster, though, outlines an egg-shaped configuration trending roughly northeast, the San Juan cluster approaches a circular one. But both clusters appear heavily forested. Basic differences include the low salinity of Lake Superior water and the lack of tides within the Apostle cluster.

After having sea kayaked in coastal British Columbia and Washington, I had to give this method of travel a try in the Apostles. With only a few days for the trip (1) in late August, and 700 miles, round trip, of driving, I sampled only three of the 22 islands and the crossings between them. But, in 21 miles, I tasted the flavor of the place. Fortunate for me, weather proved not a major challenge.

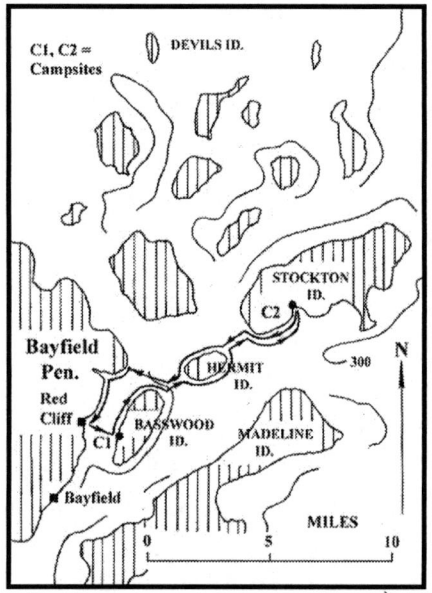

Apostle Islands and Bayfield Peninsula, Wisconsin, with route of trip 1. Wiggly lines show the 120-foot depth contours, except for the 300-foot contour near the eastern edge of the map.

As I loaded my sea kayak on the car, Ella asked, "Are you sure you want to do this? Didn't the Big Timber-Laurel trip offer you enough thrills?"

"Yes, I'm sure. And I didn't make that trip just for the thrills, but to gain more swift-water experience. Gotta try the Apostles. See how they compare with the San Juans."

"Wish you weren't going alone."

"Yeah, well. Don't know of anyone with a sea kayak who's free now."

Having arrived in Red Cliff late in the day, I chose to paddle across West Channel to the nearest campground, on the west side of Basswood Island. I trailed a 25-foot, knotted rope, a precaution as for the Big Timber-Laurel trip. A light, westerly wind aided my first crossing. I left my sea kayak just above water line, but had to carry my gear a considerable distance up a steep slope to the campground, amidst annoying mosquitoes.

After dark, a thunderstorm ushered a Fourth-of-July greeting: boisterous thunder and bright lightning flashes. Sleep came after long delay, in view of my being the only camper. I worried a bit about lightning downing a tree just above me.

The paddle from camp to Quarry Bay on Stockton Island required 2 hours and 45 minutes. I traversed the Basswood-Hermit Island crossing in 20 minutes, the Hermit-Stockton Island crossing in 25 minutes. On the Basswood-Hermit crossing, I experienced 2- to 3-foot waves, impinged by a light northwest wind. I wondered about the difficulty—or possibility—of boarding my craft upon dumping. And how long I'd last in the choppy, 50-degree F water.

I decided to camp at Quarry Bay, a delightful place with a sandy beach, on Stockton, and not proceed to other islands should the weather deteriorate.

The warm, clear day induced me to hike through dense woods to an inactive brownstone quarry at the southwest edge of Stockton Island. Owners of this quarry and others on Basswood and Hermit Islands shipped the 500-million-year-old sandstone for construction in the late 1800s to such mid-western cities as Chicago, Detroit, Milwaukee, and Cleveland.

Trees on Stockton appeared similar to those at Voyageurs National Park (trip 8), but I didn't observe yellow birches and hemlocks at Voyageurs. While I took some note of natural features at Stockton, having to return from an island loomed in the back of my mind as the day wore on.

Signs near the campground warned of black bears. I learned later that Stockton Island had one of the greatest concentrations of black bears in North America. Precaution said that food should be hung in a tree. I had no perishable food, so I simply set out granola, sealed in a plastic bag, for breakfast inside the foot of my pup tent.

The wind switched to the southwest, the direction of my return, and I could hear waves lapping onshore all night. I worried about the trip back to Red Cliff, which made my sleep fitful.

During the night, two couples, in a group tent within 15 yards of my tent, awakened me with loud, nervous conversation. "What's that noise?" asked a female voice.

"Don't know," said a male voice. "Let me get my light." Pause. "It's a damn bear," said the male voice.

"A bear!" the women shrieked.

"Calm down," said the other male voice.

"Shut up, and go to sleep," ordered the first male voice.

"Who can sleep with a damn bear almost in our tent!" shouted a second female voice.

"Did you hang our food in a tree?" asked the first female voice.

"No, it's mostly in a cooler by the tent," said the first male voice.

In the morning, I gulped my granola, and hurriedly broke camp for the trip back. But I couldn't help checking out my neighboring campers. Obvious bear tracks in the sand and droppings on the ground and on the picnic table testified to the nocturnal marauder. One male pointed to the wide-open cooler. "Damn bear figured out how to open the cooler. He snarfed up our steaks and hamburgers."

I shook my head, but lacked time to empathize, and headed directly toward my overturned craft on the beach. Once there, though, I saw a thunderstorm looming in the southwest. I sought cover, waited for it to pass, and hoped others would not appear.

A southwesterly head wind and 3-foot waves made paddling somewhat difficult, but I stroked the Stockton-Hermit Island crossing in 35 minutes. The Hermit-Basswood crossing proved easier with only 1- to 2-foot waves, and required only 30 minutes, although I passed through a rain shower. The Basswood-Red Cliff Point crossing proved easier still, and took only 20 minutes. Total time, from Quarry Bay to Red Cliff, tallied at 4 hours and 15 minutes.

Impressions: I desired to paddle the Apostles again but to visit several other islands, and preferably with a partner for safety reasons. Based on weather forecasts and my own estimates, my limits for sea kayaking here—without undue apprehension—stood at 3-foot waves and 20-knot winds. Two- to 3-foot waves and 10- to 15-knot winds would rank as more comfortable. On the next trip, I would allow more time for layover on the islands should the weather prove fickle. Stronger winds seemed to frequent the Devils Island area, so I would probably avoid the vicinity of that island. But another trip never came to pass.

Application to Life: We all take chances in life, be they adventurous, financial, or interpersonal. Sometimes the risks tread heavily, sometimes light. We must weigh the risks against the benefits. If our chances prove manageable, we rise above them the wiser. If not, we pay a price for the education.

Chapter 12
Sense of Trip Urgency

My dad, Charles, didn't understand canoes or canoeing. And to my knowledge, my mother, Lillian, never paddled a canoe, much less even sat in one. My parents visited us from Idaho when son Mark was less than a year old. I arranged for a stay at a cabin on Bad Medicine Lake in northwestern Minnesota, northwest of Park Rapids.

I took Dad for a short paddle on the lake, and all went well. His shortage of conversation, though, suggested to me that he may have felt less comfortable in a canoe than in a boat with a power motor. And the name "Bad Medicine" forebode an event later in the day.

Well into scuba diving at the time, I wished to demonstrate the process to Dad. I donned my gear, and flippered the canoe and him just offshore. "Water's real clear," I said. "You can keep an eye on me. Everything okay?"

"Yeah," he replied, with little conviction.

In 15 feet of water, I searched for freshwater mussels for about 20 minutes. Upon finishing a tank of air, I surfaced for a full one. I lifted my diving mask off my face to check on Dad, and found him nowhere in sight toward shore. I spun around to see the *bottom* of the canoe facing me. "Oh, boy," I said out loud, and power-kicked to the canoe.

On the backside of the canoe, Dad hung with an arm wrapped around the center thwart. "Musta lost my balance, lookin' in the water for you. Damn canoe just slipped away under me. Called to the women, but they didn't hear me."

They didn't hear him because of their undivided attention to baby son Mark.

I held back a smile, and pushed him home as he still hung onto the center thwart. But I had to marvel at his instinct for survival and not panicking, even to the point of recovering his soggy hat from the lake. Prudent it would be not to bring up the subject of canoes again.

By 1980, within 11 years after his dumping on Bad Medicine Lake, two milestones had passed: my mother's death, and my dad's move to a retirement home because of losing his legs–thanks to diabetes. I became more conscious of his impending death, but strove to ignore that probability.

In 1980, my desire to canoe proved stronger than in previous years, and I canoed more miles–302. I'm not sure why. Was the urgency linked to covering more river miles before my needed presence at his deathbed?

The first trip in May (trip 58), on the lower Yellowstone, I've already covered in Chapter 8. Before my family and I left for our extended annual vacation in early June, I checked in with Dad. He asked, "Do you have to go on this trip?"

I had never known him to show concern over my travel. But I cast aside his thought, and set out toward Montana.

The second trip (trip 60), in mid-June on the upper Yellowstone, I've already mentioned in Chapter 8, from below Yellowstone National Park to below Emigrant, Montana. Intermittent rain the first day made seeing shallowly submerged boulders difficult, and steady rain kept son Mark and I confined most of the second day to our pup tent.

Two days later, I took the third 1980 trip (59), the reckless, solo, 73-mile slip from Big Timber to Laurel, Montana. I've documented this trip in Chapter 11. I wondered what Dad would have said about this foolhardy dash should I have had the opportunity to describe it to him.

A short, 15-mile trip (56) in late June on the lower Yellowstone between Sidney and Fairview, Montana, I paddled jointly with by brother-in-law, Frank. He and I shared the discovery of a bison skull and elk antler buried in a cut bank of the Missouri River in 1974 near Culbertson, Montana, discussed in Chapter 9.

On the final trip (52), on July 1 and 2, Mark and I paddled 57 miles on the Missouri River from Poplar to Culbertson. We camped the first day in a cow pasture between Poplar and Brockton, a mile below where Roosevelt County 251 crosses the river. We experienced ideal paddling conditions both days—calm to westerly breezes—and averaged 4 mph. Birds along the way included cormorants, great blue herons, and pelicans but, surprisingly, no Canada geese.

On July 2, we arrived early near Culbertson, about a mile and a half southwest of town. We walked and hitchhiked into town so I could call Ella to pick us up. Fortified with a cold drink and snack, I called my brother-in-law Frank's residence in Fairview. Frank's wife, Mary, responded to my call. "I'm afraid I have some bad news for you, Alan."

"Oh?"

"Yes. Your father passed away–today. Heart attack."

Even though expected, I felt devastated by the news.

I turned to Mark. "Your grandpa died."

Mark looked at me in disbelief. "Grampa?"

"I tried to get some airplanes to find you on the river," Mary continued," but they had no luck."

I knew that I must take charge, and return home as soon as possible. "Can you put Ella on the phone?" I asked.

"I'm really sorry, Alan," said Ella.

"Yeah, thanks." I paused to dry my eyes. "Can you pick us up at the highway bridge southeast of town? It'll probably take you 45 minutes or so. We've got to hike back to the canoe and paddle a ways."

As we paddled in silence, my mind raced. *Why did Dad die while I was on a canoe trip? Could it be, in part, because of his aversion to canoes and canoeing? This seems farfetched. Did he have a premonition of his death when he didn't want me to leave town on an extended vacation trip? I should have been at his deathbed.*

When Ella arrived at the bridge, several noisy teenagers had already congregated there with booze. She felt unsafe waiting for us alone, and headed into Culbertson for the town policeman.

As Mark and I reached the take-out, I puzzled at the policeman with Ella. Was she in some kind of trouble? With my thoughts concentrated on Dad's death, I didn't need another complication. But before we loaded canoe and gear, the teenagers had left, followed by the policeman.

Application to Life: Journeying on the water can be likened to journeying through life. Few can predict what events will take place and when, well and good in the main. If we could predict with accuracy, we might be troubled much of our lives–as when waiting for impending deaths of our loved ones or our own.

Chapter 13
Post-Back-Trauma Tripping

I paddled 16 C/K trips after Dad's death until another major milestone. In January, 1989, I twisted my body in a handball game which set off lower back pain that has plagued me, off and on, since. Another book, *Back Trip: A Journey Into Perseverance*, chronicles my battle against this pain, which forced me into early retirement.

Ella and I emigrated to Wyoming in 1992. By 1997, I had worked my way back into canoeing on a limited basis. This required, in part, clamping a small boat seat with back rest to the rear seat of the canoe. And the 14 Wyoming trips through 2000, on the North Platte and Bighorn Rivers, were day trips that I've taken mostly with my special North Dakota friend, Bob. Since 2000, back-pain recurrence again placed my canoeing on hold. My sea kayak has remained in storage, unused, since 1988–still waiting for me.

I made a pilgrimage back to North Dakota in 1998 for a canoe trip with Bob in familiar water, using his canoe. This marked my fourth run of trip 31 on the Red Lake River in Minnesota. High water and many rapids accompanied us on the last day of May. To reduce the chances of damage to Bob's canoe, I elected to line his craft around several rapids. Wildflowers included Canada anemones, golden alexanders, columbines, dame's rockets, and butter-and-eggs. And we saw several birds: great blue herons, bald eagles, sandpipers, bank swallows, and various ducks.

Three trips on the North Platte in the south-central part of Wyoming (64, 65, and 66), totaling 22 miles, showed a commonality of traits. Paddle rate in September proved slow, averaging about 2.5 mph. We saw bald eagles on all three trips–and on one trip, two birds in the same tree!

And these trips provided a first for me. Many shoals over a gravel bottom necessitated that we wade and walk the canoe away from rocks to deeper water. We donned chest waders just for this purpose. A little cumbersome, to be sure, but the waders proved more than a nice-to-have accessory. We had to use caution, though, when slipping back into the canoe at the approach of deeper water. We could have ended up on our backs with waders filled with water–a nasty condition.

The Fremont Canyon trip (67), although only 9 miles long, proved overwhelming from the standpoint of scenery. This part of Fremont Canyon contains backwater of the North Platte River, dammed-up by the Alcova Dam near Alcova, Wyoming. The tail race of the Fremont Canyon Hydroelectric Power Plant at the upper end of the canyon limits further travel. Walls of the canyon, steep-sided to vertical, approach 800 feet in places. Just beyond the third major bend from the canyon's mouth, we marveled at a natural arch high up on the south canyon wall. Roughly half way up the canyon, where layered sedimentary rocks overlie granite, provides a good place to land a canoe. The granite has been dated at 2.8 billion years old. Yes, 2.8 *billion years*. Being in the presence of something so old makes me feel truly humble. Earth, itself, has been dated at 4.6 billion years.

Fremont Canyon trends north-northeast, and when paddling up-canyon, Bob and I had a light to moderate head wind from the southwest, the prevailing direction. "Should be easy going back," I said, and Bob agreed. But we learned something about paddling in canyons. Some tight bends in the canyon face *toward* the southwest. So, in such places, the prevailing wind struck the opposing canyon walls and bounced back to present a secondary head wind *against* us. Closer to the canyon's mouth at Alcova Reservoir, we erected a makeshift sail from a poncho to give us a boost.

The canyon trip took longer than normal because we measured water depths with a depth finder at five places. Water depths ranged from 122 feet near the canyon's mouth to 33 feet just below the power plant.

We saw several bird species on this trip. Among them: pelicans, turkey vultures, common mergansers, and magpies.

The roughly 42 river miles on the North Platte between Gray Reef Reservoir and Casper, I subdivided into seven trips (68 through 74), with some overlap between them. Bob accompanied me on five of the trips, his wife, Annie, on two. On trip 72, I attempted to instill a taste of canoeing into my grandson, Christopher, as he rode with my daughter, Julie, her husband, and me during a rare get together. Likely a foolish act on my part, because what would he remember at age 2 ½ ? We crossed rapids with standing waves at the point where Bessemer Mountain meets the river, called Bessemer Narrows. Christopher thrilled at the run through the rapids as his father received a lapful of water. I had some doubt as to taking my family through the rapids, but my route at the edge of the standing waves proved correct and manageable.

Our adult female friend, Lori, accompanied Ella and me on trip 74, the 9 miles from Bessemer Bend to Casper. With this trip, Ella broke her canoeing hiatus, 33 years after her first trip on the Shell and Crow Wing Rivers in Minnesota. She obviously placed a much lower priority on canoeing than I did! At the put-in, just below the mouth of Poison Spider Creek, the river splits into four channels. I steered for the right one of two middle channels, which proved a poor choice. The canoe got caught on rocks, spun around, and we headed down-river backwards. I hadn't experienced backward travel since some of my earlier canoe trips in Minnesota. But in a short distance, we whipped back to normal, and had no other mishaps. On trip 73 with Bob, similar to trip 74, I chose the left-most channel just below the mouth of Poison Spider Creek. This time, I had no difficulty with rocks or being spun around backwards.

The seven trips between Gray Reef Reservoir and Casper can be summarized as follows. Paddling rates varied from 3 to 5 mph with an average of about 4 mph. Birds seen included pelicans, Canada geese, cormorants, great blue herons, common mergansers, ospreys, kingfishers, eastern kingbirds, blue-winged teals, and sandpipers, as well as others. Mammals included mule deer, white-tailed deer, pronghorn, and a swimming muskrat with grass in its mouth. Among the trees and shrubs: cottonwoods, willows, boxelders,

Russian olives, buffaloberries, dogwoods, pincherries, skunkbushes, currants, and white clematises.

Bob, Annie, and I made a highlight sighting on trip 71. Well ahead of us we spotted what resembled a slight riffle on the water that shifted across the river, not with the current if truly a riffle.

"Could be a muskrat," offered Annie.

"Don't know about that," said Bob. "Maybe not as conspicuous as a muskrat."

"Let's beat it out!" I yelled to Bob, and we resorted to power strokes to reach the left bank at about the same time as the so-called riffle. Our efforts proved worthy. The "riffle" turned out to be the wake of a large bull snake that drew itself onto the riverbank and disappeared into the bushes as we watched.

High water on trip 71 created rapids with standing waves at the point where Bessemer Mountain meets the river, similar conditions as for trip 72. I guided the craft through an obvious downstream vee but Bob, in the bow, received a lapful of water because of the high standing waves. As mentioned earlier, the same thing happened on trip 72 with grandson Christopher and his parents.

The day after trip 71, lightning triggered a 780-acre brush fire on the southwest side of Bessemer Mountain. The fire was put out 3 days after we came down the river. We could have easily seen the burn from the river.

Trip 75 ranked as the most exciting of the post-back-trauma trips: Wendover Valley and Canyon on the North Platte River between Glendo and Guernsey Reservoirs. This trip, with Bob, began below the

Glendo Dam across the river from the power plant, and ended at Wendover above the Guernsey Reservoir. The route, which trends generally south-southeast, begins in a 400-foot-deep canyon, then passes into relatively flat terrain at Bulls Run. After a few miles, the river enters 400-foot-deep Wendover Canyon, which narrows and disappears before reaching Wendover.

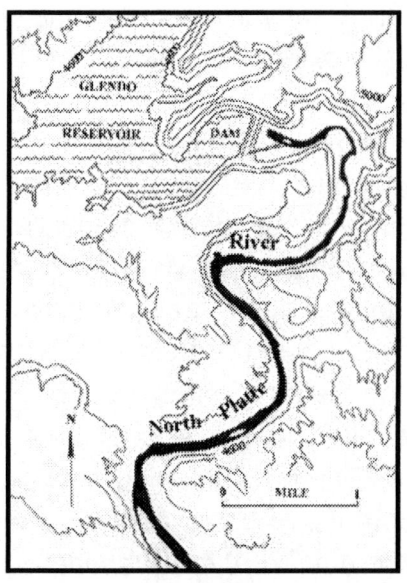

Map of North Platte River just south of Glendo Dam and Reservoir, southeastern Wyoming. Contours depict hundred-foot intervals. The canyon is 400 feet deep.

Most of the land adjacent to the river lies within private ownership. A railroad flanks the river over much of the route, and frequent trains shatter the natural silence except that of the flowing water.

Water level stood relatively high during this early September trip, with a good current, especially at Wendover Canyon where the river narrows. We experienced a paddling rate, for the 15 river miles, of 4.8 mph. We encountered four major rapids, and received water in the canoe twice. At the major rapids, I'd tell Bob: "Better get on your knees."

"Aye, aye, captain," he'd reply.

Many vegetated islands populated the river, and added to the variety of the canyon scenery.

Woody plants included ponderosa pines and junipers on the canyon slopes, and cottonwoods, Russian olives, boxelders elms, and white clematises along the river's banks.

We saw both white-tailed and mule deer. One white-tailed deer munched white clematis.

A good variety of birds snagged our interest: cormorants, Canada geese, mallards, common mergansers, blue-winged teals, kingfishers, ospreys, bald eagles, magpies, great blue herons, and sandpipers. And the highlight of the trip: wild turkeys

At Wendover we encountered a couple distractions. We heard deafening noises to the north and east, much like you'd expect in a war exchange. Then we remembered the Wyoming Army National Guard Camp near the town of Guernsey. Apparently, we had heard explosions at a bombing range. Although loaded and ready to leave Wendover, we found that a train blocked our crossing the tracks. We walked along the train cars, but saw no one. Finally we heard voices. I shouted: "Is the train going to sit here all day? How do we cross the tracks?"

"Don't worry," replied a voice on the other side of the train cars. "Drive about a mile to the southwest, and you'll be able to cross there."

Rare has it been that I've exchanged words with a body-less voice.

Bob and I paddled our last trips (62 and 63) in Wyoming on the Bighorn River in the Thermopolis vicinity. On trip 62, we paddled 8 river miles from Wedding of the Waters to Hot Springs State Park in Thermopolis in 2 ½ hours for a rate of about 3 mph. We worked against a moderate to strong wind much of the time, and in light rain part of the time.

Let's pause for an artifact of history. Lewis and Clark named the river the Bighorn, the Crow Indians called it the Wind River. To add to the confusion, some early explorers believed in the existence of two, separate waterways. But, of course, the same river bears both names. Going downstream, the Wind River becomes the Bighorn River at Wedding of the Waters.

The river presented a high level so we had almost no concern about striking rocks. Clear water enabled us to see the bottom, likely gravelly, and sandy nearshore, covered mostly with pondweeds in long streamers. Was the prolific growth of aquatic plants due to nutrients added to the water, such as from fertilizers? We passed by a few cliffs of reddish rocks that geologists place in the Chugwater Formation.

Woody plants along the banks included mostly Russian olives, wild roses, and white clematises in the fluffy seed stage.

As for birds, we observed ducks, kingfishers, turkey vultures, sandpipers, and crows.

At the take-out, I wandered to the mouth of a spring that enters the river, just upstream from the Suspension Bridge in the state park. I recalled what I witnessed at this spot 6 ½ years previously–two softshell turtles–the longest estimated at 10 inches. I had seen softshells maybe only twice before in my lifetime. Softshell turtles, described by one writer as "animated pancakes," have soft and leathery shells completely devoid of scales. No softshells in sight this time.

Trip 63 extended from the Suspension Bridge at Hot Springs State Park 12 river miles to the Black Mountain Road Access north of town on the right bank. Paddling rate remained the same as for trip 62. We had to portage around two, low diversion dams constructed of slabs of concrete and rocks.

The high water level, clear water, and presumed mostly gravelly bottom covered with aquatic plants in long streamers remained as for trip 62.

Just north of Hot Springs State Park, we spotted a few hot springs at the water's edge. At how many places can you touch flowing hot water over limy travertine while seated in your canoe? This experience ranks amongst those rare and ultra-special.

Cotttonwoods could be added to the woody plants of trip 62. Blossoming plants included nightshades (with fruit), mulleins, water speedwells, lady's thumbs, goldenrods, rabbitbrushes, and tamarisks or saltcedars.

Animals seen along the way included white-tailed deer–one mother kept two fawns up close, and a single muskrat and bull snake. As for birds, we saw kingfishers, great blue herons, sandpipers, ducks, cormorants, turkey vultures, coots, magpies, killdeers, and common mergansers.

Application to Life: You canoe/kayak to the extent that you can. If some condition limits you, you still travel within the range of your limitations. Your life's travel works the same way. Accept your restrictions with increasing age, but maintain your activities as long as you can enjoy them—especially those that hinge on the creative.

Chapter 14

Synopsis: C/K Strokes and Life's Strokes

Paddle strokes can be thought of as metaphors for life's strokes. You apply both types of strokes in small increments but which, over time, can add up to something of major significance. In Chapter 4, I discussed how various paddle strokes can relate to the acquisition of life's goals.

Each C/K stroke brings forth the unknown, often the unexpected. In like manner, each stroke in life's journey exposes the unknown, and frequently challenges you with the unexpected.

Paddle strokes require effort against a resisting force, that of the water. Life's strokes must also confront resisting forces, in the form of inadequate finances, medical handicaps, interpersonal disappointments, inherited and unwanted responsibilities, and unexpected deaths.

The concept of stroke can go beyond the similarity of paddle strokes to incremental steps along the journey of life. One can imagine the Stroke of Luck or Spirit. To some, luck plays a major role in their destiny. To others, some sort of spirit or god controls their course through life. I've thought about this a great deal. Have chronic back pain and other ailments settled in my body because I've been unlucky, or has a god willed it so? If a god's willing, was this imposed to punish me or teach me to be more empathetic of others? When wars are at stake, does the Stroke of

Luck of Spirit apply? Were some persons lucky to survive? Or did a spirit dictate who would live or die? In either case, the outcome seems uncontrollable.

Another case in the concept of stroke lies in the Stroke of Genius. A thought or idea descends on the recipient as if dropping from the sky. Genius requires superior mental power, but what helps–someone has said–is the "prepared mind": knowing how to observe, reason, and make pertinent associations.

You can also consider the Stroke of Sudden Action. Examples include a lightning strike, or with C/K travel, a capsize, whereby a sudden action requires immediate reaction.

We might include the Stroke of Intimacy as in a caress. A rather far-out meaning of stroke, but valid.

Finally, we arrive at the Stroke of Finality. This relates to death in general, or, more specifically, death by an obstruction or clot in the brain. As we often hear, he (or she) died of a "stroke."

In parting, may your paddle and life strokes be easy, may your portages be short, and may the wind most often be at your back.

A paddler slips along a quiet stream as fog lifts.

Appendix 1

CANOE AND SEA KAYAK TRAVEL LOG

Water Body	Nearest Town (s)	Water Miles	Year	C or K
Wisconsin				
1. L Superior (Apostle Islands)	Red Cliff	21	1987	K
2. Brule R	Solon Springs-Brule	17	1982	C
3. St. Croix R	Danbury	14	1976	C
4. St. Croix R	Danbury	15	1982	C
5. St. Croix R	St. Croix Falls	14	1976	C
Minnesota				
6. BWCA	Prairie Portage	15	1971	C
7. BWCA	Ely	38	1973	C
8. Voyageurs NP lakes	Ray	34	1987	K
9. Bigfork R	Effie	32	1973	C
10. Bigfork R	Big Falls-Loman	75	1978	C
11. Little Miss R	Solway	8	1981	C
12. Grant L & Crk	Wilton	4	1981	C
13. Miss R	L Itasca-Wilton	26	1974	C
14. Miss R	Wilton	7	1979	C
15. Schoolcraft R	Becida	10	1983	C
16. Schoolcraft R	Bemidji	6	1983	C
17. Miss R	Wilton-Bemidji	12	1981	C
18. Miss R	Wilton-Cass Lake	28	1972	C
19. Cass L	Cass Lake	23	1988	K
20. Miss R	Ball Club	11	1975	C
21. Miss R	Ball Club-Cohasset	25	1979	C
22. Miss R	Grand Rapids-Hassman	85	1977	C
23. Shell R	Menahga	15	1965	C
24. Crow Wing R	Akeley-Huntersville	24	1986	K
25. Crow Wing R	Huntersville-Nimrod	18	1965	C

26. Crow Wing R	Huntersville-Oylen	21	1972	C
27. Crow Wing R	Nimrod-Staples	34	1966	C
28. Clearwater R	Leonard	8	1982	C
29. Red Lake R	Red Lake-St. Hilaire	78	1971	C
30. Red Lake R	St. Hilaire-Red Lake Falls	18	1971	C
31. Red Lake R	Red Lake Falls-Huot	15	1967	C*
32. Red Lake R	Red Lake Falls-NE of Huot	10	1974	C*
33. Red Lake R	Huot-Gentilly	15	1975	C
34. Red Lake R	Gentilly-Crookston	11	1966	C
35. Red Lake R	Crookston-Fisher east	16	1972	C
36. Red Lake R	Fisher east-Fisher	8	1973	C
37. Red Lake R	Fisher-Mallory	11	1973	C
38. Red Lake R	Mallory-East Grand Forks	13	1966	C

North Dakota

39. Red River	Thompson-Grand Forks	12	1984	C
40. Red River	Grand Forks	3	1974	C
41. Pembina R	Windygates, Man-Vang bridge	16	1971	C
42. Pembina R	Vang bridge-Walhalla	12	1970	C
43. Pembina R	Windygates-Walhalla	28	1976	C
44. Heart R	Sweet Briar-	27	1972	C
45. Missouri R	Pick City-Bismarck	76	1976	C
46. Little Mo R	Medora	6	1967	C
47. Little Mo R	Medora	15	1967	C
48. Missouri R	Bainville-Williston	36	1978	C

Montana

49. Missouri R	Bainville	12	1973	C
50. Missouri R	Culbertson-Bainville	26	1974	C
51. Big Muddy R	Culbertson	5	1974	C

52. Missouri R	Poplar-Culbertson	57	1980	C
53. Missouri R	Ft Peck-Poplar	94	1978	C
54. Missouri R	Ft Benton-Landusky	150	1975	C
55. Yellowstone R	Fairview-Cartwright	20	1970	C
56. Yellowstone R	Sidney-Fairview	15	1980	C
57. Yellowstone R	Sidney-Fairview	13	1972	C
58. Yellowstone R	Terry-Buford, ND	129	1980	C
59. Yellowstone R	Big Timber-Laurel	73	1980	C
60. Yellowstone R	Miner-Emigrant	28	1980	C

Idaho

61. Pack R	Samuels	18	1970	C

Wyoming

62. Bighorn R	Thermopolis	8	2000	C
63. Bighorn R	Thermopolis-Lucerne	12	2000	C
64. N Platte R	Canyon-Saratoga	11	1999	C
65. N Platte R	Saratoga	6	1999	C
66. N Platte R	Saratoga	5	1999	C
67. N Platte R	Alcova	9	1997	C
68. N Platte R	Alcova-Clark's Corner	13	1998	C
69. N Platte R	Clark's Corner-Casper	12	1998	C
70. N Platte R	Casper	9	1997	C
71. N Platte R	Casper	6	1997	C
72. N Platte R	Casper	6	2000	C
73. N Platte R	Casper	11	1998	C
74. N Platte R	Casper	9	1998	C
75. N Platte R	Glendo-Wendover	15	1998	C

Vancouver Island, BC

76. Johnstone Strait	Telegraph Cove	40	1986	K

Washington

77. Rosario Strait	Anacortes-Eastsound	52	1987	K
78. Haro Strait	Friday Harbor	35	1988	K

River miles by state or province:

Wisconsin	81
Minnesota	754
North Dakota	231
Montana	622
Idaho	18
Wyoming	132
British Columbia	40
Washington	87
TOTAL RIVER MILES	1,965

Abbreviations:

BWCA=Boundary Waters Canoe Area
C=canoe
Crk=creek
K=sea kayak
L=lake
Miss=Mississippi
Mo=Missouri
N, NE=north, northeast
R=river